Legal Perspectives on Bridging Science and Policy

Legal Perspectives on Bridging Science and Policy deals with the interaction of science and policy from a legal perspective.

Expert contributors outline the role of law in water management and suggest solutions to make laws flexible and adaptive to changes in scientific knowledge and environmental, social and economic conditions. Each chapter addresses the topic with a different focus and offers an in-depth analysis of legal challenges related to the creation of interdisciplinary bridges, clarifying how science may be assimilated into decision-making processes and can thereby contribute to build evidence-based policies.

Legal Perspectives on Bridging Science and Policy will be of great interest to scholars of water law, water governance and environmental law.

This book was originally published in the journal *Water International*, as a special issue prepared by the International Association for Water Law (known as AIDA from its Spanish acronym https://www.aida-waterlaw.org), gathering selected papers dealing with law and governance from the XVI World Water Congress of the International Water Resources Association (IWRA) (2017).

Mara Tignino is a Reader at the Faculty of Law of the University of Geneva, Switzerland, and Lead Legal Specialist of the Platform for International Water Law at the Geneva Water Hub, Switzerland. She acts as an expert and legal adviser for states and international organizations. She holds a PhD in International Law from the Graduate Institute of International and Development Studies, Switzerland, and was a Visiting Scholar at the George Washington University School of Law in Washington D.C., USA.

Raya Marina Stephan is an international consultant in water law. She has a wide experience in projects on transboundary waters and she advises regional and international organizations. She was involved in the experts advisory group of UNESCO's International Hydrological Program to the Special Rapporteur of the UN International Law Commission, on the draft articles of the law of transboundary aquifers. She is the Deputy Editor-in-Chief of *Water International*.

Renée Martin-Nagle earned a PhD in Law from the University of Strathclyde, UK, with a focus on governance of offshore freshwater. She is Treasurer of the International Water Resources Association, President and CEO of A Ripple Effect PLC and a Visiting Scholar at the Environmental Law Institute, USA.

Owen McIntyre is a Professor and Director of the LL.M. (Environmental & Natural Resources Law) Programme at the School of Law at University College Cork, Ireland. His principal area of interest is Environmental Law, with a particular research focus on International Water Law. He has served as Chair of the IUCN World Commission on Environmental Law's Specialist Group on Water and Wetlands, and holds visiting positions at Charles University Prague, the Czech Republic; Wuhan University, China; Xiamen University, China; and the University of Dundee, UK.

Routledge Special Issues on Water Policy and Governance
Edited by:
Cecilia Tortajada (IJWRD) – Institute of Water Policy, Lee Kuan Yew School of Public Policy, NUS, Singapore
James Nickum (WI) – International Water Resources Association, France

Most of the world's water problems, and their solutions, are directly related to policies and governance, both specific to water and in general. Two of the world's leading journals in this area, the *International Journal of Water Resources Development* and *Water International* (the official journal of the International Water Resources Association), contribute to this special issues series, aimed at disseminating new knowledge on the policy and governance of water resources to a very broad and diverse readership all over the world. The series should be of direct interest to all policy makers, professionals and lay readers concerned with obtaining the latest perspectives on addressing the world's many water issues.

Legal Mechanisms for Water Resources in the Third Millennium
Select Papers from the IWRA XIV and XV World Water Congresses
Edited by Marcella Nanni, Stefano Burchi, Ariella D'Andrea and Gabriel Eckstein

Integrated Water Management in Canada
The Experience of Watershed Agencies
Edited by Dan Shrubsole, Dan Walters, Barbara Veale and Bruce Mitchell

Groundwater and Climate Change
Multi-Level Law and Policy Perspectives
Edited by Philippe Cullet and Raya Marina Stephan

OECD Principles on Water Governance
From Policy Standards to Practice
Edited by Aziza Akhmouch, Delphine Clavreul, Sarah Hendry, Sharon Megdal, James Nickum, Francisco Nunes-Correia and Andrew Ross

Urban Resilience to Droughts and Floods
The Role of Policies and Governance
Edited by Cecilia Tortajada, James Horne and Larry Harrington

Politics and Policies for Water Resources Management in India
Edited by M. Dinesh Kumar

Rural–Urban Water Struggles
Urbanizing Hydrosocial Territories and Evolving Connections, Discourses and Identities
Edited by Lena Holmes, Rutgerd Boelens, Leila M. Harris and Gert Jan Veldwisch

Legal Perspectives on Bridging Science and Policy
Edited by Mara Tignino, Raya Marina Stephan, Renée Martin-Nagle and Owen McIntyre

For more information about this series, please visit:
https://www.routledge.com/series/WATER

Legal Perspectives on Bridging Science and Policy

Edited by
**Mara Tignino, Raya Marina Stephan,
Renée Martin-Nagle and Owen McIntyre**

Routledge
Taylor & Francis Group

LONDON AND NEW YORK

IWRA

AIDA

First published 2020
by Routledge
2 Park Square, Milton Park, Abingdon, Oxon, OX14 4RN

and by Routledge
52 Vanderbilt Avenue, New York, NY 10017

Routledge is an imprint of the Taylor & Francis Group, an informa business

British Library Cataloguing in Publication Data
A catalogue record for this book is available from the British Library

ISBN 13: 978-0-367-40685-1

Typeset in Minion Pro
by RefineCatch Limited, Bungay, Suffolk

Publisher's Note
The publisher accepts responsibility for any inconsistencies that may have
arisen during the conversion of this book from journal articles to book chapters,
namely the inclusion of journal terminology.

Disclaimer
Every effort has been made to contact copyright holders for their permission to
reprint material in this book. The publishers would be grateful to hear from
any copyright holder who is not here acknowledged and will undertake to
rectify any errors or omissions in future editions of this book.

Contents

Citation Information

The chapters in this book were originally published in *Water International*, volume 44, issue 3 (April 2019). When citing this material, please use the original page numbering for each article, as follows:

Chapter 6
Forestry management and water law: comparing Ecuador and Arizona
Andrés Martínez Moscoso and Rhett Larson
Water International, volume 44, issue 3 (April 2019), pp. 337–353

Chapter 7
Factors identifying aquifers with a high probability of management success
Eric L. Garner
Water International, volume 44, issue 3 (April 2019), pp. 354–362

Chapter 8
The evolving framework for transboundary cooperation in the Nubian Sandstone Aquifer System
Elena Quadri
Water International, volume 44, issue 3 (April 2019), pp. 363–377

For any permission-related enquiries please visit:
http://www.tandfonline.com/page/help/permissions

Notes on Contributors

Douglas Aitken is a Researcher at the Center for Research in Sustainability and Strategic Resource Management in the Faculty of Engineering at the Universidad del Desarrollo, Chile.

Antti Belinskij is a Professor in the Department of Law at the University of Eastern Finland, and a Research Professor at the Finnish Environment Institute.

Camila Boettiger is Director of the Center for Regulatory Law and Business, a Professor of Environmental Law and Natural Resources, and a Professor in the Faculty of Engineering at the Universidad del Desarrollo, Chile.

Daniel Brieba is an Assistant Professor in the School of Government at the Universidad Adolfo Ibañez, Chile.

Stefano Burchi is the Executive Chairman of the International Association for Water Law (AIDA), Italy.

Roberto O. Bustillo Bolado is Professor of Administrative Law in the Department of Public Law at the University of Vigo, Spain.

Cristian Candia is a Research Assistant at the Collective Learning Group at MIT Media Lab at the Massachusetts Institute of Technology, USA, and is finishing his PhD at the Center for Social Complexity at the Universidad del Desarrollo, Chile.

Deborah Curran is Associate Professor of Environmental Studies in the Faculty of Law and School of Environmental Studies at the University of Victoria, Canada.

Guillermo Donoso is Professor of Water Economics at the Water Law and Economics Center at the Pontificia Universidad Católica de Chile.

Eric L. Garner is Managing Partner at Best Best & Krieger LLP, USA, working in water rights and supply law.

Alex Godoy-Faúndez is Director of the Center for Research in Sustainability and Strategic Resource Management in the Faculty of Engineering at the Universidad del Desarrollo, Chile.

Mauricio Herrera is Director of Basic Sciences in the Faculty of Engineering at the Universidad del Desarrollo, Chile.

Hannu Huuskonen is a Senior Researcher in the Department of Environmental and Biological Sciences at the University of Eastern Finland.

Rhett Larson is an Associate Professor at the Sandra Day O'Connor College of Law at Arizona State University, USA.

Renée Martin-Nagle is Treasurer of the International Water Resources Association, President and CEO of A Ripple Effect PLC and a Visiting Scholar at the Environmental Law Institute, USA.

Andrés Martínez Moscoso is a Professor and Researcher in the Faculty of Economics and Administrative Science, and the Faculty of Jurisprudence, Political and Social Sciences at the University of Cuenca, Ecuador. He is also a lawyer.

Owen McIntyre is a Professor and Director of the LL.M. (Environmental & Natural Resources Law) Programme at the School of Law at University College Cork, Ireland.

Laura Movilla Pateiro is a Lecturer in the area of International Public Law in the Department of Public Law at the University of Vigo, Spain.

Elena Quadri is a Research Associate at the Water Resources Research and Documentation Centre at the University for Foreigners of Perugia, Italy.

Diego Rivera is an Associate Professor in the Department of Water Resources and the Laboratory of Comparative Policy in Water Resources Management at the University of Concepción, Chile.

Niko Soininen is Assistant Professor in Sustainable Law, Regulation and Governance at the University of Helsinki, Finland, and a Senior Researcher in Environmental Law at the University of Eastern Finland.

Raya Marina Stephan is an international consultant in water law. She is the Deputy Editor-in-Chief of *Water International*.

Mara Tignino is a Reader at the Faculty of Law of the University of Geneva, Switzerland, and Lead Legal Specialist of the Platform for International Water Law at the Geneva Water Hub, Switzerland.

Anssi Vainikka is Professor of Evolutionary Aquatic Biology in the Department of Environmental and Biological Sciences at the University of Eastern Finland.

Bridging science and policy: legal perspectives

Mara Tignino, Raya Marina Stephan, Renée Martin-Nagle and Owen McIntyre

Science plays a significant role in policy decisions related to the management and protection of water resources, at both national and transboundary levels. Legal frameworks provide analytical tools to develop the linkages between science and policy and to implement science-based policies and decisions. Law and policy play prominent roles in the integration of scientific knowledge within society. However, the interrelation between law, science and policy is complex and multifaceted and pulls in two directions: importing law into science and policy while exporting science's approaches and methods to law and policy.

This volume of *Water International* represents the third special issue prepared by the International Association for Water Law (known as AIDA from its Spanish acronym; https://www.aida-waterlaw.org). AIDA is a network of legal and policy specialists active in government, academia and civil society who have a specific interest in freshwater resources law and related disciplines. It partners with a variety of inter-governmental, governmental and non-governmental institutions to ensure that water law is properly integrated in the governance of freshwater throughout the world.

Consistent with the two previous AIDA special issues (37:6, 2012, and 41:6, 2016), this volume gathers selected papers dealing with law and governance presented at the IWRA's 16th World Water Congress, held in Cancun in 2017. AIDA has played an active role as a contributor to the development of this congress by leading the delivery of the water law and governance track running through the programme, soliciting presentations from high-level legal experts, and organizing a special session on the Greening of Water Law. AIDA volunteered to have the present guest editors review the diverse submissions and identify those legal papers that were of particular significance for this special issue.

The articles selected and published in this volume deal with legal aspects of water management addressing the conference theme of 'Bridging Science and Policy'. They outline the role of law in water management and suggest solutions to make laws flexible and adaptive to changes in scientific knowledge and environmental, social and economic conditions. Each contribution addresses the topic with a different focus and offers an in-depth analysis of legal challenges related to the creation of interdisciplinary bridges. Together, this assemblage clarifies how science may be assimilated into decision-making processes and can thereby contribute to build evidence-based policies.

Burchi opens the issue with an exploration of the latest trends in the development of domestic water law through analyzing the evolving legal frameworks of countries representing different regions of the world and diverse legal systems. The trends that emerge include novel considerations in water laws, such as the emerging role of the environment, greater attention to the impacts of land-based activities on water quality and on the natural processes of water-retention, and concerns about providing proper recognition of the custom-based rights and practices of traditional and native communities. The author further identifies recently emerging trends, including the human right to water, the recognition of legal personalities in rivers, and the promotion of alternative dispute-resolution mechanisms to facilitate access to justice in water disputes.

This overview sets the scene for three papers dealing with legal aspects of water management at the national level. Looking at Canada, Curran examines the ability of provincial water laws, predicated largely on an abundance of water, to adapt to changing hydrologic conditions when there is no longer enough water to secure all water entitlements. The author notes that administrative orders regarding allocation are becoming increasingly common due to low flows or over-allocations, particularly in the west of the country. After analyzing the context of water law in Canada and of the existing legislative basis for adapting water entitlements, the author concludes that water law reform must enable planning, assessment of cumulative effects and monitoring at the basin scale, and must also include recognition of the Aboriginal rights to water.

Herrera et al. consider water disputes in Chile, where water management and allocation are based on a free-market approach and strong neoliberal influence in tradable water rights. In their paper, the authors provide a multidimensional study of adjudicated disputes involving water rights in Chile. The study shows a substantial increase of legal disputes regarding water rights, as well as clear patterns of geographic locations for these conflicts, and legal arguments and strategies used in their pursuit. The authors found also an increased diversification of the subjects contained in the legal claims over time, which suggests an augmentation in their complexity.

Bolado and Pateiro explain how water considerations affect Spanish urban planning. After decades of unsustainable growth based on property speculation and rampant construction, legislative and judicial interventions have recently mandated that proof of the existence of sufficient water resources to fulfil the estimated needs of any urban planning (new residential areas, industrial zones, etc.) must be provided before authorization for those projects may be granted.

Groundwater resources require specific management considerations, especially when they are transboundary. Garner provides key information for improving the effectiveness of aquifer management efforts worldwide. He identifies and elaborates on the factors that have led to successful management of certain aquifers, such as the Genevese Aquifer in France and Switzerland, the Los Sotillos Aquifer in Spain, the Eastern Snake Plain Aquifer in Idaho, and a number of California basins. Quadri examines the evolution of the cooperation in the case of a single, yet extensive, transboundary aquifer system, the Nubian Sandstone Aquifer System, shared by Chad, Egypt, Libya and

Sudan. She notes the importance of procedural norms in this evolution and recommends increased reliance on substantive norms in order to reach a more mature level of cooperation based on the 2008 UN Draft Articles on the Law of Transboundary Aquifers.

The issue concludes with two papers dealing with the impacts of water management on two different aspects of biodiversity: migratory fish in Finland, and forests in Ecuador and Arizona. As described by Soininen et al., migratory salmonids in Finland are today an endangered species due to extensive damming and hydropower production. The authors analyze the principal legal and scientific drivers for re-evaluating some of the existing hydropower operations in Finland. They argue that there is a need for re-estimation on the basis of legal obligations deriving from EU legislation and new scientific knowledge. Moscoso and Larson compare public–private partnerships dedicated to improving forestry management to protect water in the Paute River basin in Ecuador (FONAPA) and the Verde River basin in Arizona (the Four Forest Restoration Initiative). Both programmes create incentives for improved forestry management and suggest lessons for water management in general. But synergistic learning between the programmes is inhibited by the differences in the legal status of water and forest resources in the two systems.

The guest editors hope that this collection will provide useful new information and insights and will open new areas of research on the role that law can play to bridge science and policy. We wish you good reading and invite you to consider adding your own contributions to the emerging issues raised here. We also hope fellow legal experts will join the next IWRA World Water Congress, in Daegu, Korea, 11–15 May 2020.

The future of domestic water law: trends and developments revisited, and where reform is headed

Stefano Burchi

ABSTRACT

A re-visitation of trends and developments in water legislation in the light of experience and new legislation from selected countries confirms the findings of prior stocktaking, while bearing out advances in many areas: achieving adaptability of regulatory water-allocation mechanisms; blending efficiency and equity of allocation; 'greening' of water laws; bridging the land–water divide; and giving customary and de minimis water rights their due. The human right to water, and access to justice, are emerging new trends. These, and the advances listed earlier, show the likely direction of future water law reform.

Introduction

Water in general, and its sustainable management, are the focus of standalone Sustainable Development Goal (SDG) 6 ('Ensure availability and sustainable management of water and sanitation for all'), and relevant targets, adopted by the United Nations (UN) General Assembly in September 2015 alongside 16 other SDGs and related targets (UNGA, 2015). Water is also directly or indirectly connected to a number of SDGs, and instrumental to the achievement of their targets (Sindico, 2016). Although neither governance nor an enabling/supporting legal framework have made their way explicitly into SDG 6 or into the relevant targets, the instrumental role governance plays towards the achievement of SDG 6 and, in particular, of all the relevant targets, is readily apparent. Hence, the finding in the first World Water Development Report that the 'water crisis' is a crisis of governance has lost none of its appeal 16 years after the report was released in 2003.

Picking up from where prior comparative water law work left off (Burchi, 2011, 2012), this paper takes stock of, and revisits, salient features and trends detectable through the lens of contemporary water resources laws from a broad spectrum of countries representative of different regions of the world and of the diversity of legal systems (Appendix A carries a list of the statutes analysed by the author). The choice of countries reflects the author's personal effort to cast a net as widely as possible and to feature countries from all five continents. Following a re-visitation of the salient features and trends detectable in the contemporary generation of water laws, the issues and the challenges that emerge from this paper's consolidated comparative stocktaking are highlighted, and the likely course and direction of water law reform ahead are mapped out as a result. The analytical material that forms the bulk of this paper is organized in a logical sequence that closely mirrors the internal organization and structure of mainstream contemporary water statutes. Therefore, the narrative in this paper unfolds from the foundational pillars of water resource regulation, beginning with the legal status of water resources and followed by the regulation of water allocation, abstraction and use, before zooming in on efficiency of allocation and use and on the human rights dimension of allocation and use. The paper then moves on to the more novel features of contemporary water resource regulation, from the emerging role of the environment as a new entry in the known constellation of claimants for scarcer water to paying attention to the impacts of land-based activities on water quality and on the water-retention natural processes that occur overland and underground. The paper also examines the myriad micro-scale, custom-based water uses and users in rural areas, and access to justice in water disputes.

Re-visitation of salient features and trends in the light of contemporary water resources legislation

Water's legal status as a public property good

As attested to by a string of consistent contemporary water laws, the trend to regard water as a public property good and to place it as a result in the public domain of the state and in the scope of governmental or judicial allocation authority (Burchi, 2012) has solidified further. In a leap forward into seemingly uncharted legal territory, Japan's Water-Cycle Act (2014) refers to water as 'an asset shared by all human beings'. Whether this expression equates to humankind is an open question, with unclear legal implications (Burchi, 2015). Ecuador's new Water Act (2014) goes as far as banning the 'commodification' of water. Of note also is the expansive legal definition of water resources, which often encompasses 'non-conventional' sources, such as treated wastewater and water in the atmosphere. Exceptionally, private water havens persist, notably as regards groundwater and as a result of judicial pronouncements (Supreme Court of Texas (USA) rulings made in 2012[1] and 2015[2]), or predicated on statute that are carefully delimited in scope (Bangladesh Water Act, 2013).

Enhancing the adaptability and flexibility of regulatory instruments of water allocation

Contemporary water laws indicate that known regulatory instruments of water abstraction, that is, administrative licences and other equivalent instruments (concessions, authorizations, permits), are being made increasingly adaptable to reflect rapidly changing hydrological, hydrogeological, technological, economic and environmental circumstances, and in response to advances in scientific knowledge. In these contemporary laws, flexibility is inherent in the standard authority vested in the government water administrations to review and, if need be, adjust – also downwards – abstraction licences, with or without compensation depending on the circumstances. For example, the downwards variation of abstraction licences during their lifetime, to reflect changing stream-flow levels and water availability, features in the water laws of Ecuador (2014), Tanzania (2009) and Namibia (2013), in context with the standard authority of the respective government water administrations to review, amend, suspend or cancel abstraction licences. Under South Australia's Natural Resources Management Act 2004 as amended in 2011, water allocations for a forest development purpose may be varied, but, unlike allocations for other purposes, the volumes allocated under a 'forest water permit' can only be reduced after the forest has been harvested (Avey & Harvey, 2014[3]). Compensation for downsized licences is not mentioned in the Ecuadorian or Tanzanian laws, while it is explicitly ruled out in the Namibian law. Under Zambia's Water Act (2011), the *quantum* of permitted abstractions can be scaled down, without compensation, in three circumstances: (1) when there is the need to protect the availability of water in the source to which the abstraction permit relates; (2) when there is the need to protect a water resource, groundwater or an ecosystem from serious damage; and (3) when the variation does not reduce the *quantum* of an abstraction to below the minimum required for the particular permitted use. The role of the courts in effecting the adaptation of water abstraction rights to, in particular, changing natural environmental circumstances is noteworthy, as in the European Union (EU) under the effect of the EU Water Framework Directive (2000) (Fundación Nueva Cultura del Agua, 2008).

Shifting from fixed volumetric/flow grants towards share-based adjustable grants signals a leap forward in the same direction – and a pretty sophisticated one at that. For example, the Water Management Act, 2000 of New South Wales (Australia) abolished common law riparian water rights and replaced them with a complex administrative system of time-bound 'access licences'. Such licences are made up of two parts: a 'share component', which entitles the licence holder to shares in the available water from a given source, and an 'extraction component', which entitles the licence holder to take water at specified times, rates and at specified locations. The actual determination of the 'share component' of access licences is based on the water-sharing rules to be made with respect to each water body, what is referred to in the Act as the 'Bulk Access Regime' (BAR), which is perhaps the key feature of the entire water abstraction licensing system. A BAR, and the water sharing rules that make it up, will determine how much water will be available for extraction by each licensed water user. BARs will be based on water-sharing plans and will, like these plans, be in effect for 10 years. If changes are made to the BAR during the term of validity of the plan, resulting in a reduction in the available water for abstraction and in the downsizing of allocations under the relevant licences, compensation can be claimed by licensed water users (Burchi, 2001). Transition to a share-based system of abstraction licences is under consideration in England and Wales in the context of reforms to the system in effect. Under the new system, abstractors would receive a share in the 'available water resource' instead of an absolute amount they would be entitled to abstract. Elimination of compensation for changes to abstraction licences, now available only in certain circumstances, is also part of the reforms under consideration (Davey, 2013[4]). Elimination of the right to claim compensation now features in the Water Act 2014 of England and Wales as regards the abstraction licences held by water supply-service providers, in case they are varied by the government water administration – presumably also downwards as to the *quantum* of abstraction rights (Strategic Issues – England and Wales, 2014).

Acknowledging the human right to water

With due regard for nuances as to the actual scope and strength of the human right to water, access to water for the satisfaction of basic human needs is cast as a matter of human rights in increasing numbers of contemporary water statutes. An example is Bhutan's Water Act, 2011, which enshrines every individual's right of access to water for basic human needs. Although it is not so explicit, the statutory language has clear human rights overtones. A more compelling example is Zambia's Water Act, 2011, where the human right to water is cast as a matter of policy and principle and operationalized through the statutory priority of allocation accorded to domestic and non-commercial uses over other competing uses of water. An equally compelling example is Peru's Water Act, 2009, where access to water for the satisfaction of basic human needs (1) is also explicitly cast as a matter of human rights law and (2) is also prioritized relative to other competing uses of water. The same statute, however, goes further by directing the government to 'guarantee' access to water sources and to avoid their pollution. The new (2014) Ecuadorian dispensation also enshrines the human right to water, and it seeks to operationalize it by directing the government to set aside 'quality' water to satisfy the basic needs of present and future generations. Compliance with this direction can be demanded, presumably in the courts of law, by any person or community, within the quantitative boundaries that will be set by the water authority. Under the same new dispensation, the contours of the human right to water are further delineated by reference to the 'free and un-impeded access to surface or underground water sources for human consumption' and to a number of conditionalities that qualify the enjoyment of such access rights. Such conditionalities have regard to the quality and quantity of water, which must not be altered significantly, to the rights of third parties, which must be respected, and to equality and non-discrimination among claimants. Moreover, the government must take affirmative action in this last specific regard and pay special attention to gender.

Whereas in all the above examples it is access to raw water sources for the satisfaction of basic human needs that receives statutory attention, the human right to drinking water 'at the tap' attracts qualified attention in mainstream water legislation. This right is cast as a matter of principle, at a policy level, in the Water Act of Namibia, 2013. The Water Act of Palestine (2014) goes a step further by directing the water service providers to 'ensure' the human right of any person to drinking water of a suitable quality for his/her needs. Another notable example is Uruguay's National Water Policy Act, 2009, singling out the human right to drinking water (and to sanitation) as the foundational principle of the national water policy to be implemented through a national drinking water and sanitation plan.

Enhancing the efficiency of water allocation and use through controlled trading of water rights, charging for water abstraction and wastewater discharge, and through other means

Trading of water rights and severance of the same from land rights are becoming a popular instrument in the pursuit of efficiency of allocation of an increasingly scarce resource, notably in over-allocated basins where available water stocks are insufficient to meet competitive demands. Trading, however, tends to be subject to limitations and restrictions that account for and protect environmental, amenity and cultural values, and third-party interests. Under the Honduran Water Law (2009), for example, a water abstraction right can be mortgaged, but it cannot be traded for a use that is different from the original one. Stated otherwise, trades can only be intra- (water use) sector, and not from one sector, notably agriculture, to another, notably municipal/industrial use. Under Tanzania's Water Act, 2009, water abstraction permits can be traded with the consent of the relevant Basin Water Board. In the state of California, under the Sustainable Groundwater Management Act, 2014, the sale of groundwater extraction allocations is allowed, subject, however, to the prior authorization of the groundwater sustainability agency responsible for the aquifer.

Water rights trading is widely practised in the western states of the United States, subject to government or court approval of a transaction – something that can only be obtained if other water appropriators are not harmed (so-called 'no-injury test') (Neuman, 2004). In some countries such as Ecuador, Peru and Namibia, trading of water abstraction rights has been banned altogether. In others (Zambia), the water law makes water abstraction rights appurtenant to the land, thus effectively impeding the separate trading of water abstraction rights. Both banning water rights trading and tying water rights to land signal the lack of a uniform trend regarding the controversial issue of water rights trading.

Whereas the bulk of water rights trading involves abstraction rights, there are instances where wastewater discharge permits can also be transacted. Trading of wastewater discharge permits is contemplated, for instance, in the Water Acts of Namibia (2013) and Tanzania (2009). Water quality trading is encouraged by the US federal Environmental Protection Agency as a matter of policy and guidance (Ridgway, 2015). The legality of such trading has been challenged in court, however, albeit inconclusively (Gates, 2013).

Efficiency further underpins, overtly or by implication, the 'user pays' principle of charging for the abstraction of raw water at source – as distinct to billing for the service of delivering drinking water 'at the tap' – and the 'polluter pays' principle of charging for the negative externalities generated by the use of water bodies for the disposal of wastewater. Water resource charging is reflected in much contemporary water legislation from across the globe (e.g., Bhutan, Honduras, Peru, Ecuador, Tanzania, Uruguay, Zambia, Namibia, Palestine, state of California and Vietnam). An articulate system of abstraction charges, which includes a 'water conservation' component and contains detailed criteria for the setting of the rates of charges, is contemplated in the new Ecuadorian dispensation (2014). Charging for water abstraction and for wastewater discharge, and criteria for the setting of the relevant rates, feature also in the Water Acts of, respectively, Namibia (2013), Palestine (2014) and Vietnam (2012). Detailed criteria are provided in the Water Act of Namibia to guide the setting of the rates of charges. They are (1) the kind of resources and the method by which water is abstracted; (2) the purpose for which water is abstracted; (3) the time of the year when water is abstracted; and (4) the region of the abstraction. In the state of California, groundwater extraction fees and charges may be levied by the groundwater sustainability agencies to cover the costs of groundwater sustainability plans, programmes and to fund the cost of managing groundwater. Relevant charges can be set on a volumetric basis (Burchi, 2015).

Efficiency also underpins other mechanisms, some of which are innovative. Under the Water Act of Peru (2009), water users who invest in making an efficient use of the water they abstract and use are entitled to a rebate of applicable charges. The Act and the relevant

Regulations (2010) clarify that efficient users are also entitled to a deduction of the cost of the investment made. Such entitlement accrues from the grant by the water authorities of 'certificates of compliance' by users with government-approved water-use efficiency standards. Under the Water Act of Vietnam (2012), water users are mandated to adopt measures, techniques and technologies that promote the economic and efficient use of water resources. Moreover, investment in water-saving technology, in water reuse and recycling, in desalination, and in rainwater harvesting is encouraged through preferential tax treatment. Efficiency of use enters into the calculation of tariffs of abstraction charges levied on users of water for productive purposes under Ecuador's Water Act (2014). Finally, the termination of abstraction rights as a penalty for the hoarding of water, and the consequential release of water volumes or flows for further allocation, prescribed by the Water Act of Ecuador (2014) can be read as yet another pro-efficiency measure.

The 'greening' of water laws

The 'greening' of water laws, that is, the rising profile of the environment as a legitimate water user and claimant of a share of available water resources, has received a considerable boost by a spate of contemporary water statutes. Evidence of this is multifaceted and plentiful, ranging from environmental impact assessment/clearance requirements of proposed abstractions (provided for by the water laws of Honduras, Peru, Zambia and Bhutan) and of proposed wastewater disposal operations (as contemplated in the Water Act of Namibia) to the ecological flow requirements prescribed of watercourses (provided for by the Water Acts of Honduras, Peru, Zambia, Ecuador, Namibia, Vietnam and Bhutan). Additional manifestations of this trend range from the conservation of water-dependent ecosystems and aquatic habitats featuring on the statutory list of legitimate uses of water (Palestine Water Act, 2014) to accounting for environmental protection requirements in water resources planning (Vietnam Water Act, 2012) and for impacts on groundwater-dependent ecosystems of 'groundwater sustainability plans' (state of California, Groundwater Management Act, 2014). Other examples abound:

- Laws that accord the environmental value of water resources (Peru Water Act, 2009) and the integrity of ecosystems (Tanzania Water Act, 2009) equal standing to other competing values and pursuits, as a matter of policy and principle.
- A policy direction that human needs be harmonized with the needs of the water-dependent environmental ecosystems (Namibia Water Act, 2013).
- A requirement that allocation decisions and the relevant decision-making process consider environmental concerns in general (Honduras Water Act, 2009), including, in particular, respect for the ecological flow requirements of watercourses (Water Acts of Bhutan, Peru, Ecuador, Tanzania) and the impact of a proposed abstraction or wastewater discharge on water that has been allocated for environmental purposes and on aquatic ecosystems dependent on the water resource proposed to be abstracted (Namibia Water Act, 2013).
- Curtailment of abstraction rights to protect or restore the water-dependent ecosystems (Water Acts of Honduras and Zambia; this provision is also available in

the Water Act of Namibia with regard to well-drilling rights and to wastewater discharge permits).

- A requirement that the environment must not be harmed by a user's decision to transfer his/her abstraction right to a new user (Honduras Water Act, 2009).
- A requirement that the needs of aquatic ecosystems take precedence over other competing demands for water, in particular at times of scarcity (Tanzania Water Act, 2009; in Zambia's Water Act, 2011, the said needs rank second, right after the satisfaction of basic human needs, also in connection with sub-catchment allocation planning; in Ecuador's Water Act, 2014 they rank third).
- A requirement that environmental and sustainability criteria enter into determinations regarding the tariffs for water abstraction and for wastewater disposal charges, on a par with other criteria (Peru's Water Act, 2009, and Uruguay's National Water Policy Act 2009).
- Zoning and the consequential curtailment of abstraction rights for purposes of protecting water-dependent ecosystems (Water Acts of Bhutan and Peru), including the habitat of migratory birds (Bangladesh Water Act, 2013).
- The 'reserve', that is, setting aside a quantity of water of a quality required to, among others, protect the aquatic ecosystem and the environment in general (the concept of a 'reserve' had featured already in the National Water Act of South Africa (1998), and has been picked up by the much later Water Acts of Tanzania, Namibia, and Zambia).

Moreover, legal rights to water for the environment have begun to emerge as a category of entitlements enjoying the same features and legal protections as the legal entitlements to water for human use. Such entitlements accrue to the environment in recognition of the fact that it requires a share of available water to maintain river, lake and wetland health and to support the natural water systems on which other users depend. Environmental water entitlements may be held and managed by a dedicated new entry in the constellation of known water institutions, such as the Environmental Water Holder (e.g., states of New South Wales and Victoria, Australia) (O'Donnell, 2011).

Japan's Water-Cycle Act (2014) resonates with similar concerns for the health of freshwater systems when it acknowledges the value of a healthy and functioning hydrologic cycle to the 'global environment' and recognizes that the maintenance and recovery of a healthy hydrologic cycle is a matter of concern to 'all mankind'. The breadth of the Japanese lawmakers' concern, reaching out to planet Earth and to all people living on it, is a noteworthy and remarkable feature of the Act. The statute seems to reflect a supranational vision overcoming the national boundaries of Japan – something powerfully inspirational, whose legal implications remain unclear (Burchi, 2015). The personification of Mother Earth (*Pacha Mama*) as the holder of an original right to the conservation of water resources – a noteworthy feature of Ecuador's new water dispensation – is also powerfully inspirational. A number of ostensibly unrelated, yet relevant, behaviours and obligations prescribed of government, water users and the citizenry in the same new dispensation arguably concur in delineating and operationalizing Mother Earth's statutory right. The recent spate of individual rivers being granted legal personality, whether by parliament (the Whanganui River in New Zealand, 2017) or the courts (the Ganges and the Yamuna rivers by India's Uttarakhand State High Court, 2017; and the Atrato River by Colombia's

Constitutional Court, 2016) points in the same direction of placing the physical integrity and the ecosystemic centrality of the rivers in question atop the scale of values and interests pursued by the law. It is noteworthy that the rights that accrue to the rivers as a result of their being conferred legal personality are actually held, and can be claimed, by physical persons, or by an office, appointed as guardians (D'Andrea, 2018[5]; MacPherson & Clavijo Ospina, 2018).

Finally, water rights trading, whereby consumptive water abstraction rights can be purchased by private, non-profit entities or also by government, and redirected to in-stream use for the recovery and health of watercourses and to meet ecological flow requirements, is successfully practised in the western US states and in Australia (Garrick, 2011). To these ends, in particular, private, non-profit 'water trusts' have formed in the Western US states of Oregon, Montana and Washington and in the Columbia River Basin. In parallel, most Western US states have reformed by statute their traditional law of 'prior appropriation' and, in particular, the 'beneficial use' standard of water rights legitimacy, so that leaving water in the stream for ecological purposes now qualifies as 'beneficial use'. Such reforms effectively bypass the twin cornerstones of the law of prior appropriation dominating in those states: (1) that 'use' implies some diversion for the use of water off-stream; and (2) that non-use triggers the loss of appropriative water abstraction and use rights (Hadjigeorgalis, 2010; Szeptycki, Forgie, Hook, Lorick, & Womble, 2015).

Bridging the land–water divide

Traditionally, flood control has provided the 'space' where the connection between land and (too much) water is readily apparent and where attempts can be detected in contemporary water statutes to link the regulation of water resources development and use with land-use/town and country planning regulation. Tanzania's Water Act, 2009, reflects this approach. In Bangladesh, zoning of wetlands is an available option for flood-control purposes. Another connecting space is that of the 'diffuse' pollution of water resources, with inroads made by much contemporary water legislation to tackle diffuse pollution sources via zoning and the regulation of land-based activities, such as, notably, cropping and animal rearing (as in Namibia's Water Act, 2013). A generic direction that all land-based and underground development projects with a potential to pollute or degrade water resources must take measures to prevent and control pollution or degradation features in Vietnam's Water Act, 2012. So does another, equally generic, direction in that same statute that the application and use of pesticides and other chemicals in agriculture, animal husbandry and aquaculture must be in compliance with the norms in effect and must not cause water pollution.

Significant space for interaction comes also from the natural water recharge and discharge processes and from the influence that human activities aboveground and underground have on such processes. For instance, under the new (2009) Honduran dispensation, the loss of the naturally recharging capacity of aquifers due to urban expansion and development must be compensated for by providing gardens or other similar open spaces, presumably through the relevant town and country planning and zoning instruments or by other similar means. Under Tanzania's new (2009) dispensa-tion, consultation is mandatory between the government administrations in charge of, respectively, town and country planning and water resources as regards the zoning of land 'draining' to freshwater sources, notably, aquifers, springs and wetlands. The goal of the consultation is to inhibit land uses that are inimical to the well-being and eventual survival of these freshwater bodies. Zambia's Water Act, 2011, links catchment planning to town and country planning by directing government departments to consult with, and abide by the advice of, the water administration during the process of administering non-water legislation affecting water resources. The following laws point in the same direction, in a remarkably consistent fashion:

- A provision in Vietnam's Water Act (2012) directing that water resources planning be linked to land-use planning.
- A direction in Ecuador's Water Act (2014) that land-use/town and country planning take into account water resources plans.
- A direction in the state of California's new (2014) groundwater management dispensation that groundwater sustainability plans be formed in coordination with land-use plans and land-use planning agencies and that such plans map, among other things, the recharge area of aquifers.
- Another direction in California's new law to the effect that 'groundwater sustainability plans' be considered by local governments when contemplating certain land-use planning actions.
- A direction in Japan's Water-Cycle Act (2014) to local and national government to look to forests, farmland and urban facilities with a view to maintaining and enhancing the water storage and recharge functions in the country's watersheds.

Zoning of water resources at risk, and of designated water protection areas, for restricted land uses and land-use practices that is featured in contemporary water laws (Bhutan, Zambia, Ecuador, Namibia, Vietnam) also attests to the growing attention to the land–water interface. Zoning may trigger the curtailment of abstractions and of discharges in progress (as under Namibia's Water Act, 2013). The voluntary fallowing of cropland for the purposes of implementing the 'groundwater sustainability plans' prescribed by the state of California's new (2014) groundwater management dispensation also bears evidence of growing statutory attention to the land–water interface. Incorporating groundwater protection zones into local government land-use planning zones, successfully practised in Barbados since the 1970s (Foster & Cherret, 2014), also reflects strong integration of groundwater and land management. The land–water interface also plays itself out in relation to the protection of the sources of drinking water. Notable in this connection is Scottish Water's power under the Water Resources (Scotland) Act 2013 to enter into land-management agreements with upstream landowners. A similar approach is practised by Wessex Water and South West Water in England. Like other forms of payment to achieve good ecological water quality, the approach of the above-mentioned UK water utilities amounts to a payment for ecosystem services (Hendry, 2011).

Under South Australia's Natural Resources Management Act, 2004, as amended in 2011, statutory attention to the land–water interaction extends to capturing the impact of commercial forestry on groundwater. To this end, any change in land use from pasture to plantation forestry in specified areas that would have an impact on designated waters requires a development authorization from the environment minister, as well as a separate and additional 'forest water licence', also from the same minister. The latter licence represents the right to take a volume of water equivalent to the effect on the resource of the relevant forest type (Avey & Harvey, 2014).

In the Australian state of Queensland, mounting concern for the impacts on groundwater of growing coal seam gas extraction has resulted in the adoption of a 'Make Good Framework' (MGF), anchored in amendments made in 2010 and in 2016 to the Queensland Water Act, 2000. The MGF is rooted in the tort law principle of restoration, and it seeks to provide compensation to groundwater extraction rights holders (well owners) for the losses suffered as a result of coal seam gas extraction, in an attempt to 'make good' the harm suffered. The framework hinges on a 'Make Good Agreement' between the parties – the well owner and the mining tenure holder – outlining the respective rights and liabilities. The parties are obligated to reach agreement, and if they fail to do so, the well owner may resort to alternative dispute-resolution mechanisms. The threshold of the mining tenure holder's liability is defined by reference to a decline in the water level of an aquifer attributable to the mining activity, such that the well can no longer supply water of reasonable quantity or quality, and the decline exceeds predictive forecasts (Janjua, 2015).

Accounting for the customary water rights and practices of traditional communities

Accounting for the customary water rights and practices of traditional communities is an emerging preoccupation of lawmakers in countries with substantial native populations living by their customs and traditions in rural and peri-urban areas. Whereas such preoccupation may not go beyond some form of blanket statutory recognition of customary rights and practices (as in the Water Acts of Bangladesh and Tanzania), leaving the potential for collision with formal water rights systems intact, there is at the same time evidence of efforts made to provide more articulate statutory responses. Of particular note in this connection is the Peruvian State's undertaking to 'recognize and to respect' the native communities' water rights not only as a matter of principle but also in practice via the inalienability of such rights, their immunity to forfeiture and their priority status – presumably in the allocations made by the government water administration. The explicit reference to Convention No. 169 of the International Labour Organization (ILO) on the rights of indigenous peoples serves as a yardstick for the interpretation of the provisions of the Water Act (2009). Of note also is the state's obligation not to affect the water rights of native communities as a result of water development projects. This particular direction is of note insofar as it zooms in onto the interface between customary water rights and formal administrative water rights and, in particular, on the competition and conflict that the intersection of the two categories of water rights may generate.

To a more limited extent in view of its sweep, the Peruvian statute accords a generic priority to customary water rights. In the new (2012) Vietnamese dispensation a priority similarly accorded to ethnic minorities features among the criteria guiding governmental water allocation decisions. Similar concerns to Peru's are echoed in Tanzania's Water Act (2009), where customary rights are recognized by the statute and are granted equal status to formal rights. At the same time, however, these rights can be limited by the government as to their duration and can be subjected to the payment of charges. Bhutan's approach is somewhat different, in that the water uses practised by traditional communities, be they for livelihood or for religious purposes, are insulated from the administrative approval requirements of water utilizations under the relevant Water Act (2011). At the same time, however, such practices must be taken into account in deciding on the approval of proposed new water abstractions. Similar provisions feature in the Water Acts of Zambia and Namibia. This is precisely the point at which customary and formal rights interface and may collide, and which is in need of the most attention as a result.

Interestingly, Bhutan goes as far as codifying the otherwise loose notion of 'customary' practices and uses by reference to a kind of formal accreditation by local beneficiaries' groups, but also by reference to substantive criteria of fairness, equity and duration. In similar fashion, Ecuador's Water Authority is directed by the Water Act (2014) to record the water-related customary practices and rights of traditional communities and indigenous peoples, which bind all community members and the government water administration alike. Limited to the waters that flow through their lands, the traditional water management practices of communities and indigenous peoples, and their customs as regards the allocation of water among their members, are safeguarded by the law. Orders issued by such communities and peoples with respect to the use and allocation of water flowing past their lands are regarded as a legitimate exercise of their customary practices and rights. However, except for a direction that, in the water abstraction permitting process, the water authority respects and preserves the locations where traditional communities practise water-based rituals and observe their cultural values and practices, the points of interface and potential collision of customary water rights with formal water rights escape the Ecuadorian dispensation's cone of attention (Burchi, 2015). Of note in this context is also the mandatory representation of traditional communities in the catchment-level water administration of Zambia, in the river basin committees of Bhutan and in the apex government water administration of Peru.

Access to justice in water disputes

The ordinary courts, or, exceptionally, specialized water tribunals, are the place where disputants over water seek a solution to their disputes. In New Zealand, for instance, disputes concerning water rights are dealt with by specialist environmental courts. The US state of Colorado has a specialist water court; in South Africa there is a water tribunal operating under the Water Act, 1998 (Hodgson, 2006). A water tribunal is also provided for by the Water Act of Namibia (2013) to hear appeals from government decisions. Recourse to alternative dispute-resolution mechanisms, notably mediation and conciliation, is encouraged by increasing numbers of contemporary water laws (e. g., Bhutan, Ecuador, Namibia, Zambia) as a means of resolving water disputes locally, and of improving access to justice as a result. Recourse to these dispute-resolution mechanisms is contemplated by the 2010 and 2016 amendments to the Queensland (Australia) Water Act, 2000 as a means to expedite reaching a 'Make Good Agreement' between a well owner and a coal seam gas extractor, aimed at compensating the former for the groundwater (quantity and quality) losses suffered from the latter's activities (see above) (Janjua, 2015). Operational details are provided in some water laws. Recourse to mediation and arbitration is encouraged by the Water Act of Ecuador, and public records are kept of awards rendered as a result. The Water Act of Namibia (2013) provides for mediation as an alternative mechanism to resolve disputes with private parties and with the government. Relevant operational details are also provided as regards selection of the mediator, the privileged status of discussions and submissions made in the course of the proceedings – that is, their non-usability in court unless the parties agree – and the expenses of the mediator which shall be borne by the parties to the dispute. The Bhutanese Water Act (2011) directs that alternative dispute resolution shall be administered locally by the local water users' association or by local government and that the settlement arrived at shall be enforceable in court. Resolution of a dispute by the concerned community where the dispute occurs is also encouraged, notably by Zambia's Water Act (2011).

Underlying issues, and pointers for the future of water law reform

The above comparative analysis bears out a number of issues that make up the thread of much contemporary water legislation, the direction and purpose of which appear to be driven by the urge to respond to those issues and are compounded by the pressure generated by climate variability and by advances in scientific knowledge. The principal issues that underlie the bulk of contemporary water laws, and that will likely inform and inspire the agenda of water law reform ahead, can be articulated as outlined below.

Reconciling security of water resources tenure with risk and uncertainty

The security of water abstraction and use rights tenure, sought notably by investors, needs to be reconciled with changing circumstances such as advances of scientific knowledge, and, in particular, climate variability. This issue underpins the quest for flexibility and adaptability of administrative instruments of water allocation and abstraction, pursued by contemporary water laws through the mechanisms and the approaches illustrated above, some of which are quite sophisticated. For example, limiting the downwards variability of volumes allocated under a 'forest water permit' to after the forest has been harvested, as directed by the Australian state of South Australia's natural resources management legislation, is justified by the need to provide certainty to forest managers who are obliged to plan their activities years ahead and are not as free to modify or adapt their water requirements as other water users (Avey & Harvey, 2014). The issue of compensation of affected abstraction rights and of relevant allocations looms large in this context, with no uniform response emerging as regards, in particular, downsizing the *quantum* of abstractions; some laws duck the issue altogether, and others either call for or rule out compensation. Some courts, for example, in Spain (Fundación Nueva Cultura del Agua, 2008), have also had their say, notably as regards compensation for the imposition of environmental safeguards on water abstractions in progress (see below).

Pursuing opportunities for efficiency gains, without neglecting equity

In an environment dominated by dwindling water stocks and by the effects of climate variability, efficiency in the allocation, reallocation and use of scarce water resources is a legitimate concern, destined to command priority attention as the quality and quantity of available water stocks come under stress. As illustrated above, several measures – regulatory and non-regulatory – found in contemporary water laws bear testimony to the quest for efficiency of allocation and reallocation. The tradability of rights for water abstraction and wastewater disposal, fees for abstracting raw water at its source, and varying rewards for efficient user behaviour all evidence efficiency concerns as regards allocation of a scarce resource and the conveyance of waste. Contemporary water laws, however, also disclose that efficiency tends not to come at the expense of social and environmental equity. This is evidenced by the regulatory limitations imposed on the trading of water (abstraction) rights to protect a third party's interests and to protect intangibles such as environmental, amenity and cultural values. The freedom of small to micro-scale (also termed *de minimis*) abstractions from administrative licensing requirements and from regulatory controls, which is generally predicated on grounds of administrative expediency, carries – if only by implication – strong equity overtones in resource allocation. Tellingly in this regard, Peru's Water Act (2009) predicates the freedom accorded small and micro-scale abstractions on grounds of 'social equity'.

Arguably, however, insulating small to micro-scale abstractions from regulatory attention, also in the name of equity, is a double-edged sword, for insofar as they escape the radar screen of regulatory legislation, such abstractions are deprived of the legal protections that accrue to regulated, formal rights. As a result, they are exposed to erosion by formal rights and risk becoming lower priority rights (Hodgson, 2016; van Koppen, Schreiner, & Sithole, 2018). If these rights do fall within the reach of regulatory legislation, notably of legislation imposing regularization formalities on small-scale abstractions falling above a minimum threshold for total exemption (as in the current water laws of Kenya, Malawi, Uganda, Zimbabwe and Nicaragua), such abstractions run a very high risk of being penalized, if not criminalized altogether, if they fail to comply with the prescribed formalities. The net result can hardly be described as equitable, or one that fosters peaceful coexistence between different categories of water abstraction and relevant rights, particularly when – as is often the case – compliance failures by users are attributable to the limited capacity of governments to implement water laws. This phenomenon has been documented in Southern Africa (van Koppen et al., 2018) and Central America (Munk-Ravnborg, 2016, documents the experience of, in particular, Nicaragua). Where small to micro-scale abstractions are legalized by a stroke of the statutory pen, limited or partial implementation leads to much the same result by creating water abstraction outcasts, who are mainly irrigators. A notable example of this is South Africa's Water Act, 1998, which requires compulsory licensing of existing lawful uses under both the Water Act and the general authorizations mechanism whereby all small-scale users that the government cannot reach with permits should be covered by a general authorisation. Van Koppen et al. (2018) and Kidd (2016) document attempts to implement the compulsory licensing provisions of the South African Water Act in selected basins, with mixed success.

Reconciling the environment-support function with the development-support function of water resources, and repositioning water at the centre of the ecosystem

The environmental requirements of freshwater bodies, and those of water-dependent habitats, increasingly compete for statutory attention and standing with development needs. The process, known as 'greening' of water laws, is evidence of such competition and of the tension between the environment- and development-support functions of water resources. Greening also attests to the consistent effort of contemporary water laws to reposition water at the centre of the ecosystem and to acknowledge water's ecosystem services-generating value. The recent statute- or case-based grants of legal personality to individual rivers (New Zealand, Colombia, India), and the statutory recognition of Mother Earth as the holder of water conservation rights (Ecuador) also attest to a greening of water laws. Reconciliation of these seemingly conflicting functions can be painful and costly insofar as it may involve the review and adjustment of water abstraction rights and of relevant allocations and may trigger the issue of compensation, as documented in Spain under the operation of the Water Act, 2001 and under the influence of the EU Water Framework Directive, 2000 (Fundación Nueva Cultura del Agua, 2008).

As experience in the US Western states and in Australia suggests, these pains and problems can be alleviated when the market is allowed to step in and effectively substitute, albeit not entirely, for command and control by government. A market-dictated price tag will account, and compensate for, the trade-offs involved when 'development' water for use off-stream is redirected to in-stream use for an environmental purpose through the agency of private non-profit entities or by government action. Opportunities to bridge water's developmental and environmental/ecosystemic divide are built into statutes integrating separate strands of legislation, such as South Australia's Natural Resources Management Act 2004, amended in 2011. Another notable example is the Dutch Environmental Planning Act, scheduled to enter into force in 2018, which brings together under one roof a number of policy domains, notably water management and environmental protection, in addition to spatial planning (Gilissen et al., 2015[6]).

Connecting water resources and land-use regulations and their administration

Awareness of the influence of land-based human activities on water resources, surface and underground alike, is making inroads into contemporary mainstream water legislation. In particular, the mechanisms illustrated above for coordination of the legislation regulating the development and use of water resources in general, and of groundwater in particular, with the legislation governing town and country planning and urban and rural development, are destined for increasing uptake in mainstream water legislation. Coordination of legislation will require the separate branches of government that administer, respectively, the water laws and the town and country planning laws to interface and interact with a view to improved, consistent decision-making. A notable relevant example is the formal consultation of regional water management boards in municipal spatial planning for flood risk management purposes under Poland's Water Act, 2001 and Spatial Planning and Development Act, 2003 (Gilissen et al., 2015).

Coordination can be built in legislation that is integrated across the land–water divide, as in South Australia under the Natural Resources Management Act, 2004 as amended in 2011. The Act regulates the water resources impacts of land uses, including in particular the groundwater impact of new forest developments, by a mechanism of interaction between the water abstraction permit system and the land-use approval system, whereby a 'forest water licence' complements a land development authorization (Avey & Harvey, 2014). As noted above, another notable example is the Dutch Environmental Planning Act, scheduled to enter into force in 2018, which brings together a number of policy domains, notably water management and spatial planning as well as environmental protection (Gilissen et al., 2015). The land–water interface is an area of water legislation (and of town and country planning and urban and rural development legislation) that shows progress and bodes well for a future where consistent substantive and procedural requirements are woven into the fabric of both sets of laws, aimed at protecting water resources from man-made interferences originating above- or underground and at impacting on water quality and on water volumes/flows and on the relevant natural processes.

Defusing the potential for collision and conflict between customary and statutory water rights, and fostering a peaceful coexistence of the formal and informal systems of water allocation and use

Customary water-allocation and use systems governing small to micro-scale water uses, mostly in the rural and peri-urban areas of many developing countries in Africa, Asia and Latin America, have attracted, at best, the benign neglect of mainstream water resources legislation. Yet, as competition for a scarce resource heightens, the customary water rights and practices of traditional communities are bound to come under stress from the growing appetites of home and overseas investors. Opportunities for conflict between the customary and the formal water-allocation and use systems will likely multiply as a result. This is an area of mainstream water legislation that has been coming under increasing attention and is showing already considerable innovation and dynamism in the search for mechanisms to accommodate traditional systems in the fold of statutory dispensations and to facilitate their coexistence alongside statutory systems of water resources allocation and use. Certain mechanisms hold much promise in the desired direction of peaceful coexistence of the formal with the informal systems of water rights such as the inalienability of custom-based rights, their immunity to forfeiture, the priority status they are accorded in the allocations made by the government water administration, and the reckoning with the customary rights and practices of traditional and native communities in the administrative process that leads to the grant or refusal of proposed new formal water abstraction licences or wastewater discharge permits. Still, legitimate doubts linger on, particularly when it comes to customary rights that risk criminalization under the circumstances illustrated above (van Koppen et al., 2018). Arguably, as it is impossible to defuse the potential for conflict entirely, the effectiveness of the innovative instruments posited by the latest generation of water laws will only be gauged by actual practice on the ground.

Acknowledging and ensuring the human right to water

Access to raw water at source for the satisfaction of basic human needs as a matter of (human) right – separate but complementary to access to drinking water delivered at the tap – has progressed from the most authoritative international pronouncements (UNGA, 2010[7]) and from international and regional legal instruments (WaterLex, 2017) and made its way both explicitly and implicitly into the constitutional charters of some countries (WaterLex, 2014), and into the contemporary mainstream water legislation of an increasing number of countries (WaterLex, 2014) as a matter of law and/or policy. The contours of the right, and its operationalization on the ground through administrative and/or judicial action remain open issues, however. Operationalization issues have been explored at length and in great depth (see de Albuquerque 2014, from the state's perspective; and IWA 2016, from the water and sanitation service provider's perspective). Moreover, experience on the ground has been on the rise, to the point where emerging operational 'best practices' could be distilled and documented (WaterLex, 2014). The extent to which these examples may have influenced the emerging response in the contemporary water laws reviewed above is, however, speculative.

Improving access to justice in water disputes, and simplifying and expediting the dispute-resolution process

Improving access to justice in water disputes and simplification of the dispute-resolution process through community-level resolution of water-related disputes and through recourse to alternative dispute resolution mechanisms are clearly discernible emerging trends. Access to justice is a growing area of attention in mainstream water legislation that does not do away with or bypass the role of the ordinary or specialized courts of law as the place where water disputes are addressed and settled, since ultimate recourse to these legal fora remains available to dissatisfied disputants. Rather, the emerging trend attests to the lawmakers' willingness to facilitate the resolution of water disputes with minimum disruption and expense to the litigants, thereby minimizing opportunities for overt, long drawn-out, socially disruptive and expensive conflict. Recourse to ADR mechanisms and to community-level dispute resolution opens up new opportunities in the pursuit of justice in the field of water, far from the intricacies, uncertainties, duration and costs of formal litigation in the courts of law, whose distance from the location of the dispute complicates access to water justice for litigants who live and use water in the rural and in the peri-urban areas.

Conclusions

A re-visitation of the earlier comparative water law analyses by this author (see the Introduction) in the light of contemporary water laws and experience confirms earlier findings:

- The public-good legal connotation of water resources, with isolated pockets where private groundwater persists.
- The rising profile of the environment and of the ecosystem in the regulation and management of water resources in rivers, lakes and aquifers, which heralds a shift of regulatory attention from water as predominantly a factor of economic and social development towards water's ecosystem-centric position and role. As a result, the integrity of water bodies and of the ecosystems depending on them ranks atop the scale of societal values and interests pursued by those water laws.
- The perception of water as a scarce resource calling for efficiency of allocation and reallocation and for in-stream use for environmental conservation purposes.

- An awareness that land and water interface at points of regulatory intersection and that they need to be regulated in a coordinated and consistent fashion.
- A concern that the custom-based rights and practices of traditional and native communities populating much of the rural and peri-urban areas must not be neglected in formal water dispensations.

It is noteworthy that these findings permeate the Brasilia Declaration of Judges on Water Justice, adopted at the 8th World Water Forum (Brasilia, 18–23 March 2018) (Brasilia Declaration).

Some more recent trends are also emerging:

- The human right to water, particularly raw water at the source.
- Conferment of legal personality to rivers (and to Mother Earth).
- The promotion of alternative dispute-resolution mechanisms and of relevant locally based administration as a means to facilitate access to justice in water disputes and to simplify and speed up their resolution.

Re-examination also discloses some significant advances with respect to the human right to water, the status of customary rights in water and the regulated allocation of water resources. In particular, a shift is detectable in the attention to detail in the delineation and/or operationalization of matters of policy and principle, such as the human right to water 'at source' and the recognition of customary water rights on the ground. Without detailed provisions and active implementation, these matters of policy and principle run a high risk of having inspirational value only and of remaining a dead letter in practice. The increasing flexibility and adaptability of regulatory instruments of water allocation to change is also noteworthy in this context. Advances on this particular score have been influenced by advances in the scientific knowledge of natural water-related processes and of human impacts on them, feeding the policy debates and consequently informing science-based legislative responses (Avey & Harvey, 2014, documenting precisely this in the context of the water law reform experience of the state of South Australia).

As a final note, bestowing legal personality on entire freshwater bodies, notably on rivers or on Mother Earth, in recognition of water's life-giving and spiritual attributes lies at the cutting edge of legal thinking on the foundational role of water, whereby the physical integrity and the ecosystemic centrality of water and water bodies are positioned atop the scale of values and interests pursued by the law.

Notes

1. *Edwards Aquifer Authority v. Day*, judgment delivered 24 February 2012. For a discussion, see http://aquadoc.typepad.com/waterwired/2012/02/jesse-j-richardson-jr-opines-summary-of-the-e-a-a-v-day-case.html/.
2. *Edwards Aquifer Authority v. Bragg*, judgment delivered 1 May 2015. The court interpreted the Day case and applied it to the facts of the Bragg case (for a discussion, see https://agrilife.org/texasaglaw/2015/05/04/texas-supreme-court-will-not-hear-bragg-v-edwards-aquifer-authority/). In the event, the case concluded in 2016 when, on remand, the jury in the trial court issued a judgement for US$2.5 million (exclusive of interest) in favour of the Braggs as compensation for the taking of their groundwater right. Sometime afterwards, the Edwards

Aquifer Authority announced it would not appeal the verdict and would pay the judgment, totalling US$4.5 million when interest was added.

3. Avey and Harvey report that a similar approach was, at the time of their writing, under consideration in fellow Australian states of Victoria and Western Australia.
4. Davey observes that reforms are not expected to come on stream until about 2020.
5. D'Andrea reports that the Uttarakhand High Court ruling, made in March 2017, was stayed in July 2017 by India's Supreme Court on a petition by the State of Uttarakhand made on a number of legal and administrative grounds (e.g., a single Union State cannot be responsible for a river that flows to other Union States beyond its borders). In the United States, a similar attempt was made to have the Colorado River declared as a legal person in court. The case, filed in September 2017 in a federal court (*Colorado River Ecosystem/Deep Green Resistance v. the State of Colorado*) was eventually withdrawn by the plaintiff in the face of stiff opposition (including the threat of sanctions) from the Colorado Attorney General's Office. D'Andrea further reports that Canada is looking into granting legal personality to Lake Winnipeg; and that the Australian state of Victoria has recognized by statute in 2017 the Yarra River as 'one living and integrated natural entity'. The relevant statutory recognition, however, has fallen short of acknowledging the river as a legal person.
6. Gilissen et al. note that all countries in their review (Belgium, France, the Netherlands, Poland and the UK) 'have implemented some formalized form of advisory or consulting mechanisms similar to the Dutch and Flemish "water test"' (p. 26). For such a 'water test', see Burchi (2012).
7. This Resolution was followed by the UN Human Rights Council Resolution A/HRC/Res/18/1 of 28 September 2010, 'The Human Right to Drinking Water and Sanitation'. Subsequently, on 17 December 2015, the UN General Assembly adopted by consensus Resolution A/RES/70/169, recognizing 'the human right to sanitation' as a separate and distinct right to the right to drinking water.

Disclosure statement

No potential conflict of interest was reported by the author.

References

Avey, S., & Harvey, D. (2014). How water scientists and lawyers can work together: A 'down under' solution to a water resource management problem. *Journal of Water Law, 24*(2), 45–61.

Brasilia Declaration of Judges on Water Justice. (2018, March 21). Retrieved from https://www.iucn.org/sites/dev/files/content/documents/brasilia_declaration_of_judges_on_water_justice_21_march_2018_final_as_approved_0.pdf

Burchi, S. (2001). Year-end review of comparative international water law developments. *Journal of Water Law, 12*(6), 330–337.

Burchi, S. (2011). 2009–2011 year-end review. *Journal of Water Law, 22*(6), 248–265.

Burchi, S. (2012). A comparative review of contemporary water resources legislation: Trends, developments and an agenda for reform. *Water International, 37*(6), 613–627.

Burchi, S. (2015). 2012–2014 year-end review. *Journal of Water Law, 25*(5), 224–242.

D'Andrea, A. (2018) Can the river spirit be a person in the eye of the law? *International Water Law Project Blog*. Retrieved from https://www.internationalwaterlaw.org/blog/2018/03/26/can-the-river-spirit-be-a-person-in-the-eye-of-the-law/.

Davey, C. (2013). Consultation on reforms to the abstraction licence system (Strategic Issues – England and Wales). *Journal of Water Law, 23*(5), 199.

de Albuquerque, C. (2014). *Realizing the human rights to water and sanitation. A Handbook by the UN special Rapporteur Catarina de Albuquerque*. Bangalore, India: Precision Phototype.

Retrieved from http://www.ohchr.org/_layouts/15/WopiFrame.aspx?sourcedoc=%
2FDocuments%2FIssues%2FWater%2FHandbook%2FBook1_intro_%2Epdf&action=view

Foster, S., & Cherret, J. (2014). *The links between land use and groundwater – Governance provisions and management strategies to secure a 'sustainable harvest'*. Global Water Partnership (GWP). Retrieved from https://www.gwp.org/globalassets/global/toolbox/publica tions/perspective-papers/perspective_paper_landuse_and_groundwater_no6_english.pdf

Fundación Nueva Cultura del Agua. (2008). *La revisión ambiental de las concesiones y autorizaciones de aguas* [The environmental revision of water concessions and authorizations]. Zaragoza: Brufao Curiel, P.

Garrick, D. (2011). *Water markets and institutional innovations to govern environmental flows in the Western U.S.* Global Water Forum (GWF) Discussion Paper 1101. Canberra, Australia: GWF. Retrieved from http://www.globalwaterforum.org/2011/07/19/871/

Gates, A. (2013). A swing and a miss – The first reported challenge to water quality trading is dismissed for lack of standing (US litigation and regulation: Selected issues). *Journal of Water Law, 23*(5), 193.

Gilissen, H. K., Alexander, M., Beyers, J. C., Chmielewski, P., Matcak, P., Schellenberger, T., & Suykens, C. (2015). Bridges over troubled waters: An interdisciplinary framework for evaluating the interconnectedness within fragmented flood risk management systems. *Journal of Water Law, 25*(1), 12–26.

Hadjigeorgalis, E. (2010). Incorporating the environment into the market: The case of water trusts and environmental water transfers in the Western United States. *Wessex Institute of Technology (WIT) Transactions on State of the Art in Science and Engineering, 37*, 107–121. Southampton, UK: WIT Press. Retrieved from https://www.witpress.com/Secure/elibrary/ papers/9781845644062/9781845644062008FU1.pdf

Hendry, S. (2011). Strategic Issues – Scotland. *Journal of Water Law, 22*(6), 279.

Hodgson, S. (2006). *Modern water rights – Theory and practice*. FAO Legislative Study 92. Rome: FAO

Hodgson, S. (2016). *Exploring the concept of water tenure*. FAO Land and Water Discussion Paper 10. Rome: FAO

International Water Association (IWA). (2016). *Manual of the human rights to water and sanitation for practitioners*. London: Author.

Janjua, R. (2015). Mitigating water impacts in coal seam gas extraction: Is Queensland's 'Make Good' framework a suitable regulatory model? *Journal of Water Law, 25*(5), 211–223.

Kidd, M. (2016). Compulsory licensing under South Africa's national water act. *Water International, 41*(6), 916–927.

MacPherson, E., & Clavijo Ospina, F. (2018). The pluralism of river rights in Aotearoa, New Zealand and Colombia. *Journal of Water Law, 25/6*, 283–293.

Munk-Ravnborg, H. (2016). Water governance reform in the context of inequality: Securing rights or legitimizing dispossession? *Water International, 41*(6), 928–943.

Neuman, J. C. (2004). The good, the bad, and the ugly: The first ten years of the oregon water trust. *Nebraska Law Review, 83*(2), 432–484. Retrieved from https://digitalcommons.unl.edu/ nlr/vol83/iss2/7

O'Donnell, E. (2011). Institutional reform in environmental water management: The new Victorian environmental water holder. *Journal of Water Law, 22*(2/3), 73–84.

Ridgway, M. H., Jr. (2015). New tools for water quality trading. *Journal of Water Law, 25*(3), 142–143.

Sindico, F. (2016). *Transboundary water cooperation and the sustainable development goals*. UNESCO-IHP Advocacy Paper. Paris: UNESCO

Strategic Issues – England and Wales. (2014). *Journal of Water Law, 24*(2), 77.

Szeptycki, L. F., Forgie, J., Hook, E., Lorick, K., & Womble, P. (2015). *Environmental water rights transfers: A review of states laws*. Stanford, CA: Water in the West and National Fish and Wildlife Foundation. Retrieved from https://waterinthewest.stanford.edu/sites/default/files/ WITW-WaterRightsLawReview-2015-FINAL.pdf

United Nations General Assembly. (2010). Resolution A/RES/64/292 of 28 July 2010 'The Human Right to Water and Sanitation'.

United Nations General Assembly. (2015). Resolution A/RES/70/1 of 25 September 2015 'Transforming our world: The 2030 Agenda for Sustainable Development'

van Koppen, B., Schreiner, B., & Sithole, P. (2018). Decolonizing peasants' marginalisation in African water law. *Journal of Water Law*, *26*(2), 51–59.

WaterLex. (2014). *National human rights institutes and water governance: Compilation of good practices*. Geneva: Author. Retrieved from https://www.waterlex.org/new/wp-content/uploads/2015/02/WAT-Compilation_online.pdf

WaterLex. (2017). *The human rights to water and sanitation – An annotated selection of international and regional law and mechanisms*. Geneva: Author. Retrieved from https://www.waterlex.org/new/wp-content/uploads/2017/12/Waterlex_HRWS-Publication_EN_Final.pdf

Appendix A: Laws analysed by the author

The laws cited to in the work of other authors, listed under the References section, are not listed here. The text of all laws listed below are on file with the author

Bangladesh – Bangladesh Water Act, 2013 (Act No. 14 of 2013)
Bhutan – The Water Act of Bhutan 2011
California (USA) – Sustainable Groundwater Management Act, 2014 (California Water Code, Division 6, Part 2.74)
Ecuador – Organic Law on Water Resources, Uses and Abstraction of Water, No. SAN-2014–1178 of 31 July 2014
Honduras – Law on Waters, Decree No. 181–2009 of 30 September 2009
Japan – Basic Act on the Water Cycle Policy – Act No. 16 of 2014
Namibia – Water Resources Management Act, 2013 (Act No. 11 of 2013)
Palestine – Decree No. 14 of 2014 Relating to the Water Law
Peru – Law No. 29.338 of 30 March 2009 on Water Resources
South Africa – National Water Act, Act No. 36 of 1998
Tanzania – Water Resources Management Act, No. 11 of 2009
Uruguay – Law 18.610 of 2 October 2009, carrying the Principles for a National Water Policy
Vietnam – Law No. 17/2012/QH13 of 21 June 2012, on water resources
Zambia – Water Resources Management Act, No. 21 of 2011

The adaptation potential of water law in Canada: changing existing water use entitlements

Deborah Curran ⓘ

ABSTRACT
Recommendations to extend water law reform to include the adaptation of existing water entitlements goes against a basic principle of water law: to provide security of tenure to water authorization holders so they can rely on a specific volume of water. This paper evaluates how well subnational water law in Canada permits adaptive management to address existing water authorizations. With some laws allowing changes based on new scientific information, the public interest or planning, possibilities for adaptive water law in Canada arise that are instructive for other jurisdictions.

Introduction

One of the hallmarks of climate change is wider variations in hydrology (Intergovernmental Panel on Climate Change, 2007), with some scholars noting that stationarity in relation to water is dead (Milly et al., 2008). All levels of government are addressing how greater extremes in seasonal precipitation will affect the environment, economies and communities. In Canada, hydrological cycles are changing significantly, with southern basins in the west of the country, in particular, predicted to experience water deficits (Dibike, Prowse, Bonsal, & O'Neil, 2017). For the prairie provinces of Alberta, Saskatchewan and Manitoba that rely on glaciers for base flows in the major river basins such as the South Saskatchewan, flow reductions over the next 50 years are predicted to be drastic (Sandford, 2017).

Law, as the basis of water management and use, is called upon to adapt (Arnold, 2014; Bruch & Troell, 2011). However, this call for adaptation goes against one of the basic and enduring historical principles of water law: to provide security of water entitlement for users (Garner, 2016; Rose, 1990). Perversely, the tension created by heightened risk and uncertainty due to changing ecological conditions that undermine water security can lead to a greater focus on guaranteeing fixed water entitlements rather than creating water management regimes that are capable of addressing underlying ecological uncertainty in transparent and fair ways. An example of this entrenchment of existing rights was demonstrated in submissions to the Water Act Modernization process in the province of British Columbia (British Columbia Cattlemen's Association, 2013; Business Council of British Columbia, 2011).

Law reform must, therefore, become more complex as it addresses both ecological health as well as security of water entitlement in the face of hydrological uncertainty (Burchi, 2012). This includes reclaiming water for the environment in over-allocated watersheds or where there is no longer enough water to satisfy all values. Unless future management sees the construction of extensive water storage facilities capable of handling low precipitation cycles that endure for more than three years, water regulators, typically national and subnational governments, will need to adapt water entitlements over time as ecological conditions change. Adaptive water law includes not only just changing the way that water authorization holders use water but also adapting the existing entitlements that authorize water use.

Over the past 20 years in Canada, some discrete subnational law reforms, primarily in the province of Alberta, have addressed adaptation (Bankes, 1995, 2010; Percy, 2004). However, to date, there has not been a systematic analysis of the ability of provincial water law to adapt to changing hydrological conditions when there is no longer enough water to provide security of water entitlement. The purpose of this paper is to evaluate whether subnational water law in Canada provides for adapting existing water authorizations in response to changing ecological and social conditions. What follows is a cursory overview of the literature on water law and adaptation, and a brief description of the context of water law in Canada, emphasizing that scientific information gaps and aboriginal and treaty rights permeate the waterscape across Canada. The remainder of the paper sets out the legislative basis for adapting water entitlements, from shorter licence terms to altering licences 'in the public interest'. It is limited to an evaluation of provincial water law as the provinces have authority for water and water law through the constitutional division of power in Canada.[1] The paper is also limited in scope to water authorizations for surface water, although in some provincial legislative regimes there is an overlap between regulation of surface water and groundwater.[2] This attention to surface water does not address authority in the public health realm to make orders and to limit activities that may harm drinking water sources. This paper only addresses the ability of provincial decision-makers to amend existing water entitlements to a defined quantity of water through a provincial water authorization. Although there are many discrete opportunities for amending or cancelling existing water authorizations, it is clear that no province takes a systematic or comprehensive approach to planning, monitoring and adapting water use.

Adaptation in water law

A theme flowing through legal scholars' exploration of adaptive management in a variety of contexts from administrative law to resource management is that traditional legal approaches are not flexible enough to allow for meaningful adaptation (Arnold, 2014; Craig & Ruhl, 2014). This is due to the reliance of environmental law regimes on an ecological steady state (Craig, 2010; Milly et al., 2008) and to the inflexibility of laws to respond adequately to environmental change (Pahl-Wostl et al., 2007).

Lack of stationarity and certainty of water availability have fundamental implications for law as most water law has been preoccupied with granting entitlements to the use or flow of a volume of water. This entitlement is based on a point-in-time assessment of ecological conditions that does not assess cumulative water uses or hydrologic trends.

The common expression of water law as granting water-use authorizations rarely revisits those initial licences to assess the impact of that use on ecosystem health. The question of whether a new use is appropriate is front-end loaded at the time of the application for a water authorization. There is rarely an opportunity to assess the impact of a law granting entitlements to a specified volume of water and to adapt those entitlements to changing socioecological conditions. Water law has not adequately considered its ability to change entitlements or to mandate the feedback loop of learning by doing (Walters & Holling, 1990).

Adaptive management directs water law to include multiple approaches such as integrated water resource management, impact assessment, reallocation of water rights, increases in efficiency, water pricing and markets, conditions on new authorizations, and monitoring (Bruch & Troell, 2011). It is law that pays attention to appropriate scales (Ebbesson & Folke, 2014) and will, to a large extent, challenge many of the basic premises upon which law is based, chief of which is certainty (Ruhl, 1997). Some scholars predict that the necessity of adaptation will result in the merging of water, land use and environmental law, with a concurrent evolution in property law relating to elements of ecosystems not yet regularly privatized (Ruhl, 2010).

The call for reallocating water rights and for monitoring addresses the global issues of over-allocation and changing hydrology. Several sophisticated regulatory jurisdictions have resorted to buying back water entitlements from water authorization holders. For example, in Australia, one phase of the drastic water law and policy reforms in the Murray–Darling Basin included a budget of AUD 3 billion to buy back existing water authorizations (Wittwer, 2011). Likewise, in the United States, non-profit organizations called water trusts either lease or purchase water rights and leave the water instream to augment environmental flows. One study from over a decade ago cited the cost of US $75–600 per acre foot, equivalent to 1,233,482 million litres, to purchase water rights (Neuman, 2004). Given the US dollar value of these purchases and the predicted scale of climate change impacts, it is unlikely that governments around the world will be able to afford such sweeping reallocation of public funds to private entities in compensation for reductions in the entitlement to use water, which is a public resource.

In the Canadian context, subnational governments have significant regulatory space to shape how water is used. Legally, water authorizations are a use entitlement that can be changed over time as each province exercises some ability to adapt water authorizations. However, none ties adaptation to the planning–implementation–monitoring feedback loop or cumulative effects assessment at a watershed scale.

Water and law in Canada

Canada is the second largest country in the world by area. Its water laws, as some of its earliest laws, followed colonial settlement, focusing on providing security of entitlement to water. These laws also provided a mechanism for resolving disputes over water by creating priority of water use or the right to continued quantity and quality. Although flowing from the riparian rights doctrine and enacted beginning in the late 1800s and early 1900s, these rules are still largely in place today, with Saskatchewan and Quebec being the only provinces to have significantly changed how entitlements to use water endure over time (Brandes & Curran, 2017; Percy, 1988).

The size of Canada means its landscape encompasses many types of hydrologic regimes and precipitation patterns. For example, the water laws in British Columbia must have the capacity to address desert-like conditions (the Okanagan Valley) and also coastal temperate rainforest (the south-west coast) located just 400 km from one another. Most of the population lives along the southern border, yet most of the water in Canada flows north and is inaccessible for agricultural and domestic uses (Sprague, 2007).

There are four systems of water law in Canada (Brandes & Curran, 2017). In the west, British Columbia, Alberta and Manitoba rely on prior allocation where security of water entitlement flows from the date an authorization holder acquires a licence or permit. This means that the older the authorization, the more secure the water entitlement because in times of shortage the more recent licence holders must restrict their water use before more senior licensees. Most other provinces use modified riparian regimes where riparian rights still endure but are supplemented by licensing of water-use activities. Saskatchewan and the northern territories have created administrative agencies and boards to deal with water allocation. Uniquely, Quebec's water law is grounded in its civil code, which stems from the French legal origins in that province (Civil Code of Québec, 1991, article 913).

Generally, in Canada provincial governments assert ownership over water, which includes the responsibility for managing its use. Water-use entitlements flow from provincial government water authorizations or riparian rights, which makes the ability to divert water subject to the rights of other riparian owners. Water allocation in Canada is a right to use water; it is not a property right (Lucas, 1990). The Canadian constitution does not protect property rights, therefore provincial governments have significant latitude to regulate water use, which includes amending water-use entitlements as directed by legislation (Curran, 2014). Except in some unique situations, water management largely occurs by provincial governments granting water entitlements and then issuing short-term orders to mitigate acute impacts when ecological conditions change, such as in drought years. Finally, some provinces, such as British Columbia, have a legacy of perpetual licences that have no end date and thus offer no simple way to revise water-use rights under them. Others, such as Ontario and Quebec, have such high thresholds (i.e., 50,000–75,000 litres per day) for triggering the requirement to obtain a water authorization that many uses go unregulated. Although provincial governments have considerable regulatory discretion, these policies make existing water law in Canada somewhat unresponsive to changing ecological conditions.

In addition, two underlying conditions burden water law in Canada. First, it is widely acknowledged that provincial governments in Canada manage water with inadequate scientific information, and there is little monitoring of ecological conditions (Fort Nelson First Nation v Assistant Regional Water Manager, 2015; Council of Canadian Academies, 2009, 2014; Hurlbert & Montana, 2015; Kreutzwiser, de Loe, Durley, & Priddle, 2013; Moore, Shaw, & Castleden, 2018). No provincial laws protect minimum environmental flow needs (Curran, 2017; Kwasniak, 2010; Nowlan, 2012), and groundwater science and regulation are inadequate (Council of Canadian Academies, 2009; Nowlan, 2005). The Environmental Appeal Board in British Columbia overturned a water licence issued for hydraulic fracturing because it was 'not supported by scientific precedence, appropriate modelling or adequate field data' (Fort Nelson First Nation, 2015, para. 337), and consultation with the affect First Nation was insufficient.[3]

The second condition is that since 1982 the Canadian constitution has recognized and affirmed aboriginal and treaty rights (Constitution Act 1982, s 35). However, no provincial government recognizes aboriginal and treaty rights to a specific allocation of water, except as expressed in the very few modern treaties (Curran, 2017; Phare, 2009). Although provincial governments consult with First Nations about development activities that will have an impact on their rights, these efforts are ineffective in ensuring continued healthy water quality and quantity in the broader traditional territories on which many First Nations rely (Garvie, Lowe, & Shaw, 2014/15; Moore, Von der Porten, Castleden, 2017; Passelac-Ross & Buss, 2011).

Given changing hydrological regimes due to urbanization, natural resource use and climate change, it is noteworthy that no provincial regime contains enforceable standards for minimum environmental flows. There is little ability to adapt licences or entitlements to water over time, and there is still a dearth of hydrological science informing decision-making about water use except in some special watersheds. In addition, none of these regimes acknowledges aboriginal rights to water, nor factor treaty or aboriginal rights to water into the water balance of any watershed if not already captured as part of the provincial licensing system. It is within this somewhat weak governance and management context that the ability to adapt water authorizations is evaluated.

Subnational approaches to adaptation in Canada

Absent large-scale buyback, amending existing water authorizations will be a key part of adaptive water management. The ability of a subnational government to change the amount of water existing licensees are permitted to use creates possibilities for iterative approaches to rationalizing water use with ecological conditions. In Canada's constitutional framework, unilateral provincial action to amend or cancel permits without incurring significant financial liability is possible because of the legal view of water as a use right that is subject to provincial law (see Table 1 for the specific legislative references for each province).

In this paper, unilateral action means provincial decision-makers amending water authorizations in response to changing hydrologic or social conditions. What is not included in this definition is cancelling or amending permits or licences because the authorization holder contravened a licence condition or regulation. All provincial water laws enable the cancellation or amendment of permits under specific circumstances, particularly if the permit holder uses water for an unauthorized purpose, fails to comply with terms or conditions of the authorization or water law, or fails to pay a water rental or fee. Likewise, what is not included in the ability to amend is making orders for immediate or short-term action, such as ceasing taking water or altering a work, that does not result in the provincial decision-maker decreasing the amount of water authorized to be taken in future. See, for example, the extensive order-making authority under sections 88 and 91–94 of the British Columbia Water Sustainability Act 2014, including in response to low flows that threaten fish (British Columbia, 2015). In contrast to this authority to amend based on misbehaviour or short-term acute conditions, this part of the paper sets out the ability in provincial law to adapt water authorizations permanently in response to low flow conditions that arise because there is no longer adequate water in a system, or because additional science has allowed decision-makers to understand better the hydrological profile of the watershed and its water sensitivities and vulnerabilities.

Examining provincial regimes across Canada reveals several opportunities for water licence adaptation: at licence renewal; with as failure to make beneficial use of water or where water is no longer needed; holdbacks with transfer of licence; pursuant to comprehensive review or plans; in the public interest; and in consideration of additional information (see the summary provided in Table 1). Finally, as discussed below, some provinces have chosen to address the question of liability for damages caused by the administrative decision to amend or cancel licences.

Licence renewal

Some provinces limit the term or duration of a water authorization such that the decision-maker can review conditions and the quantity of allocated water at regular intervals. Both Nova Scotia and Quebec limit water authorizations to a 10-year duration, while Manitoba limits authorization terms to 20 years.

Failure to make beneficial use or where water is no longer needed

Most provinces permit the amendment or cancellation of a water authorization if the authorization holder fails to make beneficial use of the water, such as in British Columbia, or where the water regulators deem that the authorization holder no longer needs the water, such as in Saskatchewan, Manitoba and Newfoundland. In British Columbia, the new water law defines beneficial use to include using water as 'efficiently as practicable' (Water Sustainability Act 2014, s. 1).

Holdback with transfer of licence

The Alberta Water Act explicitly provides for the holdback of up to 10% of the volume of a licence when the provincial government approves a water licence transfer as part of the limited water market authorized under a water management plan or by the provincial cabinet (political executive) (Water Act 2000, ss. 82, 83). The holdback must support protection of the aquatic environment or the implementation of a water conservation objective.

Pursuant to a comprehensive review or plans

Only two provinces – British Columbia and Quebec – provide for amendment to water authorizations based on comprehensive licence or activity review and watershed planning. In British Columbia, after 2044, which is 30 years after the new water law came into force, the provincial government may begin conducting licence reviews. The decision-maker may consider the following factors when conducting a licence review:

- The best available technology and best practices for water-use efficiency and water conservation.
- New information regarding actual stream flow and aquifer conditions.
- The effects of climate change.
- The licensee's beneficial use of the water.
- The use, operation or maintenance of works.
- Other relevant factors.

Following a review, the decision-maker may amend the terms and conditions of the licence to promote more efficient use of the water, including reducing the rate of diversion and requiring more efficient practices (Water Sustainability Act 2014, s. 23).

Also in British Columbia, the provincial government may adopt all or part of a water sustainability plan by regulation that mandates changes to water licences, including reducing the maximum quantity of water that a water authorization holder may divert from a specified stream or aquifer and also cancelling licences (Water Sustainability Act 2014, s. 79). Under the Quebec Water Resources Protection Act, the provincial government may identify hydrological units for water master planning purposes, and, in particular, an integrated management plan for the St Lawrence River Basin 2009 (ss. 14, 15). In addition, under the Environment Quality Act 2018, the provincial government must conduct an assessment of the cumulative impacts of water withdrawals and use on the ecosystem of the St Lawrence River Basin every five years or where the cumulative water loss from the basin equals 190 million litres per day in excess of the last assessed withdrawal volume.[4]

Public interest

Most provinces permit the amendment or cancellation of existing entitlements in the public interest or where there will be harm to the environment. The legal language used is 'on [the director's] own initiative' in Ontario (Ontario Water Resources Act 1990, s. 34.1), 'in the public interest' in Saskatchewan (The Water Security Agency Act 2005, s. 54) and Quebec (Environment Quality Act 2018, s. 31.79.1), and 'necessary for the protection of the environment' in Prince Edward Island (Watercourse and Wetland Protection Regulations, ss. 5, 6). Alberta permits amendments for significant environmental effects, public safety or in emergencies (Water Act 2000, ss. 43, 55, 64).

Additional information

Several provinces permit amendments when new information, particularly scientific information, comes to light. Nova Scotia allows amendments when 'new or corrected information respecting an adverse effect' is introduced (Environment Act 1994–95–, s. 58A). In Newfoundland, the province may amend water authorizations when an adverse effect that was not 'reasonably foreseeable' at the time it granted the authorization has occurred or may occur (Water Resources Act 2002, s. 49). Quebec's law mentions the need to take climate change and the precautionary principle into account alongside economic development, the needs of municipalities, protection of the aquatic environment and the rights of existing users when considering water authorizations (Environment Quality Act 2018, s. 31.76).

Table 1. Summary of water authorizations in Canada and their adaptability.

Province (from west to east) and law	Type[a] and duration of water-use authorizations	Description[b] and adaptability
British Columbia; Water Sustainability Act 2014	Licence	Required to divert and/or use water from a stream (s. 7) May be amended if water is not used beneficially upon review after 30 years of the Act coming into force or under a water sustainability plan (ss. 1, 23, 30, 79) No compensation for the effects caused by a change in authorization (at s. 121) unless a reduction is identified under a water sustainability plan or by regulation (ss. 74, 134)
Alberta; Water Act 2000	Licence	Required to divert and use water (s. 49) May be cancelled or suspended for emergencies, public safety or significant adverse effects on the aquatic environment (ss. 43, 55, 64) May holdback 10% upon water licence transfer under a water plan or provincial direction (ss. 82, 83) Must compensate for losses that are the result of a cancellation or an amendment for adverse environmental effects (s. 158)
	Registration	Owners of land who used a water source on their own property for agricultural purposes before 1 January 1999 are required to register their water use, but are not required to obtain a licence (s. 73)
Saskatchewan; The Water Security Agency Act 2005	Licence	Required to use water (s. 50) May be cancelled or suspended if water is no longer needed or it is in the public interest (ss. 53, 54) Must compensate for the actual value of works (s. 54)
Manitoba; The Water Rights Act n.d.	Licence, 20 years (s. 5)	Required to use or divert water for any purpose (s. 5) May be amended or cancelled if water is no longer needed, is in the public interest or to allocate to a higher priority use (ss. 14, 15, 19) Must compensate if reallocated to a higher priority use (s. 14)
Ontario; Ontario Water Resources Act 1990	Permit	Required for persons taking more than 50,000 L of water per day, but not for domestic purposes or water for livestock/poultry less than 379,000 L per day (s. 34) May be amended or revoked at the discretion of the director (s. 34.1)
Quebec; Environment Quality Act n.d.	Authorization, 10 years (s. 31.81)	Required for water withdrawals where the flow rate is 75,000 L per day or more (ss. 22(2), 31.75) May be amended or cancelled in the public interest (s. 31.79.1) Assess the cumulative impacts of water withdrawals and consumptive uses in the St Lawrence Basin every five years (s. 31.102)
New Brunswick; Clean Water Act 1989	Permit	Required for water withdrawals (s. 15)
Nova Scotia; Environment Act 1994-95	Approval, 10 years – Approval and Notification Procedures Regulations, s. 11	Required for withdrawing or diverting water where the flow rate is 23,000 L per day or more, or for storing water of 25,000 cubic metres or more (s. 5A) May be amended on the receipt of new information relating to an adverse effect, or if an adverse effect does or may occur (ss. 58, 58A)
Prince Edward Island; Environmental Protection Act 1988; Watercourse and Wetland Protection Regulations n.d.	Licence or permit	Required to remove water from a watercourse (s. 2) May amend for the protection of the environment (ss. 5, 6)
Newfoundland and Labrador; Water Resources Act 2002	Licence	Required to divert, use or impound water (s. 14) May be amended or cancelled in emergencies in favour of a higher priority use if one is aware of an adverse effect that was not reasonably foreseeable at the time the permit was issued, and if water is no longer needed (ss. 15, 19, 49, 82) Must compensate if reallocated to a higher priority use (s. 15)

Note: [a] Listed are only non-temporary water-use authorizations if a province allows for more than one type of water-use authorization that can be for different durations. Water users may need other permits or authorizations to bring about the diversion of water, for example, to construct works or to carry out activities in or adjacent to a water body. See, for example, of the Water Sustainability Act 2014 (s. 11) or the New Brunswick Clean Water Act 1989 (s. 15).
[b] Each province typically lists exceptions to these blanket requirements for authorizations. For example, in British Columbia a licence is not required for domestic purposes, extinguishing a fire, testing the quality or quantity of water or conducting a flow test, or prospecting for a mineral (Water Sustainability Act 2014, s. 6).

Compensation for amending water entitlements

A few water laws make express provision for whether the provincial government will compensate water authorization holders for loss or damage related to amending, specifically reducing, their volume of water entitlements for public interest reasons. British Columbia clearly states that no compensation is owed when the government orders amendments to water authorizations (Water Sustainability Act 2014, s. 121) and provides exceptions for circumstances identified by regulation or under a water sustainability plan (ss. 134, 74). Conversely, Alberta mandates the payment of compensation to licensees for any losses incurred as a result of the amendment or cancellation of a water licence for environmental purposes (Water Act 2000, s. 158). Saskatchewan requires compensation for the value of works used in water diversions (The Water Security Agency Act 2005, s. 54). Water laws in Newfoundland and Manitoba require the provincial governments to compensate water authorization holders when they cancel a licence to reallocate the water to a higher use (Water Resources Act 2002, s. 15; The Water Rights Act n.d., s. 14).

In summary, while each province has some mechanisms to alter water authorizations, none takes a systematic approach to planning, monitoring and adapting water use. Indeed, some provinces have such high-volume thresholds to trigger licensing, such as Ontario and Quebec, that the water management regimes cannot regulate the cumulative impact of many ongoing uses. No province has performance-based or objective standards directing a decision-maker about when to adapt water authorizations 'in the public interest' or for 'protection of the environment'. Shorter licence terms, such as in Quebec and Nova Scotia, permit a review of individual authorizations more regularly than found in other provinces; however, there is no legal direction to conduct strategic or regional cumulative effects assessment on a watershed- or aquifer-wide basis unless a permitting process is large enough that it undergoes a provincial environmental assessment. Finally, the 'use it or lose it' principle that most provincial laws embrace creates a regulatory threat that perversely encourages wasteful use of water. Absent systematic review, and monitoring and reporting from water authorization holders, proving that a single permit holder is or is not using its full entitlement is legally challenging.

British Columbia has recently created the ability to take a more systematic approach to licence evaluation and planning by enabling licence review anytime 30 years after the Water Sustainability Act comes into force, coupled with the ability to develop water sustainability plans in designated areas. These adaptive approaches are stronger than what laws in other provinces enable because the legislative water sustainability planning regime in British Columbia permits the provincial government to adopt parts of plans by regulation, which can create legally binding obligations for decisions made about land use, water quality and water allocation, as well as amend specified existing water licences. For example, the provincial government can make a plan binding on a decision-maker, restrict the use of land or natural resources, or amend water licences pursuant to a plan (Water Sustainability Act 2014, ss. 76, 78, 79). However, while the plans can dictate adaptation for specific licences, the province has yet to initiate a single planning process and the 30-year delay in the ability to review licences prevents immediate and preventative action.[5]

On its face, the most promising provincial legal approach is Quebec's treatment of the St Lawrence River Basin, where the minister must conduct an assessment of the cumulative impacts on the environment of the water withdrawals and consumptive uses in the basin every five years. This ongoing evaluation provides a baseline against which decision-makers can justify amendments to water authorizations in the public interest or for protection of the environment.

Conclusions

Water law in Canada is still largely reliant on an abundance of water. Conflicts over water use are relatively infrequent, and short-term administrative orders address acute watercourse- or aquifer-specific shortages. No province has comprehensively amended existing licences in over-allocated watersheds. Administrative orders are increasing, at least in western Canada, due to low flows (British Columbia, 2015; Curran, 2017) or over-allocated conditions (Bow, Oldman and South Saskatchewan River Basin Water Allocation Order, 2007). Unlike in the Murray–Darling Basin in Australia (Curran & Mascher, 2016) or the Klamath Basin in the United States (Doremus & Tarlock, 2008), where water law regimes or the authorization holders and other interested parties themselves have updated water use under authorizations, water law's adaptation potential in Canada has not been tested at a watershed or basin scale. This assessment is consistent with the state of water law and management internationally (Bruch & Troell, 2011), but considerable potential exists for law reform given the regulatory flexibility afforded by the Canadian constitutional and subnational legal regimes.

Taking lessons from scholars in other areas of environmental management, water law reform for adaptation must enable planning and cumulative effects assessment and monitoring at a watershed or basin scale (Gibson, Doelle, & Sinclair, 2016; Sabatier et al., 2005; Sinclair, Doelle, & Duinker, 2017). Through planning, monitoring and adapting, water law and management can mature to an adaptive policy cycle that is responsive to changing hydrologic and social realities at appropriate scales (Ebbesson & Folke, 2014; Craig & Ruhl, 2014). This may require devolving planning and some decision-making from the subnational to a hydrological scale, as occurred in the Murray–Darling and Klamath basins. It may also require basing water authorizations on a percentage of available seasonal flows, rather than a fixed entitlement, as flows fluctuate more widely, as governments have implemented in the Murray–Darling Basin Plan (Horne, 2017).

In the Canadian context of unacknowledged aboriginal and treaty rights to water, it is clear that indigenous communities expect provincial governments to adapt water law regimes to include planning, cumulative effects assessment and recognition of aboriginal rights to water (Curran, 2017, Forthcoming; Garvie et al., 2014/15; Moore et al., 2017). While several provincial water law regimes enable watershed planning, the very few plans in place do not address indigenous–settler water allocations (Curran, 2015; Unger, 2009). Therefore, adaptation in water management in Canada must be equally responsive to ecological imperatives caused by a changing climate and reconciliation between indigenous and settler societies still burdened by colonialism.

Notes

1. The analysis does not address water law in the three northern territories in Canada because the water law and governance arrangements in the territories derive, in part, from land claim

agreements between the federal, territorial and First Nations governments. This provides the water boards and governing agencies with additional affirmation derived from the Constitution Act 1982 (s. 35), as described below, which is distinct from provincial water law regimes. In addition, the territories do not have independent constitutional status from the federal government, even if there is currently a process of devolution of province-like powers from federal to territorial governments.

2. The choice of explicitly limiting this analysis to surface water was for ease of reporting as authorizations to use groundwater are often entwined with well drilling standards. Approximately 70% of Canadians rely on surface water (Council of Canadian Academies, 2009). Note that Prince Edward Island has a new Water Act, passed in 2017, but it has not yet been brought into force by regulation.

3. The term 'First Nation' refers to the rights holding political organizations of indigenous peoples in Canada, with indigenous peoples being the original inhabitants. 'Aboriginal' is a term used in the Canadian Constitution Act, which acknowledges and affirms rights for Aboriginal, Metis and Inuit Canadians. Indigenous peoples include all those terms.

4. The purpose of this portion of the law is to implement the Great Lakes–St Lawrence River Basin Sustainable Water Resources Agreement, being a multilateral subnational agreement between provinces in Canada (Ontario and Quebec) and states in the United States (Illinois, Indiana, Michigan, Minnesota, New York, Ohio, Pennsylvania and Wisconsin) located in the Great Lakes Basin (s. 31.88).

5. The provincial government and the five First Nations of the Nicola watershed signed a Memorandum of Understanding on 23 March 2018, agreeing to work together on a watershed pilot project to 'develop and recommendations for a governance approach to sustainably manage water resources within the Nicola Watershed', which could include a water sustainability plan.

Acknowledgements

Special thanks to Andrew Mendelson and Erin Grey for comprehensive research assistance.

Disclosure statement

No potential conflict of interest was reported by the author.

Funding

This work was supported by the Social Sciences and Humanities Research Council [grant number 890-2015-0115] and the British Columbia Real Estate Foundation [grant number 2016-11].

ORCID

Deborah Curran ⓘ http://orcid.org/0000-0002-6014-0553

References

An Act to affirm the collective nature of water resources and provide for increased water resource protection, SQ 2009, c 21, s 1. Chapter C-6.2.

Arnold, C. A. (2014). Adaptive water law. *University of Kansas Law Review, 62*, 1043.

Bankes, N. (1995). Water law reform in Alberta: Paying obeisance to the 'lords of yesterday' or creating a water charter for the future. *Resources, 49*, 6.

Bankes, N. (2010). Policy proposals for reviewing Alberta's water (re)allocation system. *Journal of Environmental Law and Practice, 20*, 81–126.

Bow, Oldman and South Saskatchewan River Basin Water Allocation Order. 2007. Alberta Regulation 171/2007.

Brandes, O., & Curran, D. (2017). Changing currents: A case study in the evolution of water law in Western Canada. In S. Renzetti, & D. Dupont (Eds.), *Water policy and governance in Canada* (pp. 45–67). New York: Springer.

British Columbia. (2015, September 2). Ministry of forest, lands and natural resource operations news release: Water use reduction order reinstated for coldwater. Retrieved from http:\\news.gov.bc.ca/releases/2015FLNR0263-001430

British Columbia Cattlemen's Association. Submission to the Province of British Columbia on the *Water Sustainability Act* Legislative Proposal. November 15 2013.

Bruch, C., & Troell, J. (2011). Legalizing adaptation: Water law in a changing climate. *Water International, 36*, 828–845.

Burchi, S. (2012). A comparative review of contemporary water resources legislation: Trends, developments and an agenda for reform. *Water International, 37*, 613–627.

Business Council of British Columbia, 2011. Submission to the Province of British Columbia on the *Water Sustainability Act* Policy Proposal. March 14 2011.

Civil Code of Quebec, CQLR c CCQ-1991, article 913.

Clean Water Act, SNB 1989, c C-6.1.

Constitution Act, 1982, being Schedule B to the *Canada Act 1982* (UK), 1982, c 11.

Council of Canadian Academies. (2009). *The sustainable management of groundwater in Canada – expert panel on groundwater*. Ottawa, Canada: Author.

Council of Canadian Academies. (2014). *Environmental impacts of Shale gas extraction in Canada*. Ottawa, Canada: Author.

Craig, R. K. (2010). 'Stationarity is dead' – long live transformation: Five principles for climate adaptation law. *Harvard Environmental Law Review, 34*, 9–73.

Craig, R. K., & Ruhl, J. B. (2014). Designing administrative law for adaptive management. *Vanderbilt Law Review, 27*, 1.

Curran, D. (2014). British Columbia's water sustainability act – A new approach to adaptive management and no compensation regulation. The University of Calgary Faculty of Law Blog on Developments in Alberta Law. Retrieved from http://ablawg.ca

Curran, D. (2015). Water law as a watershed endeavour: Federal inactivity as an opportunity for local initiative. *Journal of Environmental Law and Practice, 28*(1), 53–87.

Curran, D. (2017). Leaks in the system: Environmental flows, aboriginal rights and the modernization imperative for water law in British Columbia. *University of British Columbia Law Review, 15*(2), 233–291.

Curran, D. (Forthcoming). Hydraulic fracturing in Canada: Regulation by moratorium or specialized agencies in landscapes of aboriginal and treaty rights. In J. McKay, E. Lopez-Gunn, R. M. Buono, & C. Staddon (Eds.), *Regulating water security in unconventional gas and oil*. New York: Springer.

Curran, D., & Mascher, S. (2016). Adaptive management in water law: Evaluating Australian (New South Wales) and Canadian (British Columbia) law reform initiatives. *McGill Journal of Sustainable Development Law, 12*(2), 174–227.

Dibike, Y., Prowse, T., Bonsal, B., & O'Neil, H. (2017). Implications of future climate on water availability in the western canadian river basins. *International Journal of Climatology, 37*(7), 3247–3263. Retrieved from https://doi.org/10.1002/joc.4912

Doremus, H., & Tarlock, A. D. (2008). *Water war in the Klamath Basin: Macho law, combat biology, and dirty politics*. Washington, DC: Island Press.

Ebbesson, J., & Folke, C. (2014). Matching scales of law with social–ecological contexts to promote resilience. In A. S. Garmestani & C. R. Allen (Eds.), *Social–ecological resilience and law* (pp. 265–292). New York: Columbia University Press.

Environment Act, SNS 1994–95, c 1.

Environment Quality Act, 2018 CQLR c Q-2.

Environmental Protection Act, RSPEI 1988, E-9.

Fort Nelson First Nation v. Assistant Regional Water Manager (2015) BC EAB Decision, 2012-WAT-013(c), 3 September 2015.

Garner, E. L. (2016). Adapting water laws to increasing demand and a changing climate. *Water International, 41*, 883–899.

Garvie, K. H., Lowe, L., & Shaw, K. (2014/15). Shale gas development in Fort Nelson first Nation Territory: Potential regional impacts of the LNG boom. *BC Studies, 184*(Winter), 45–72.

Gibson, R. B., Doelle, M., & Sinclair, A. J. (2016). Fulfilling the promise: Basic components of next generation environmental assessment. *Journal of Environmental Law and Practice, 29*, 257.

Horne, J. (2017). The politics of water reform and environmental sustainability in the Murray–Darling Basin. *Water International, 42*, 1000–1021.

Hurlbert, M. A., & Montana, E. (2015). Dimensions of adaptive water governance and drought in Argentina and Canada. *Journal of Sustainable Development, 8*, 120–137.

Intergovernmental Panel on Climate Change. (2007). *Climate change 2007 impacts, adaptation, and vulnerability.* Cambridge: Cambridge University Press.

Kreutzwiser, R. D., de Loe, R. C., Durley, J., & Priddle, C. (2013). Water allocation and the permit to take water program in Ontario: Challenges and opportunities. *Canadian Water Resources Journal, 29*(2), 135–146.

Kwasniak, A. (2010). Instream flow and Athabasca oil sands development: Contracting out/waiver of legal water rights to protect instream flow – A legal analysis. *Alberta Law Review, 48*, 1–33.

Lucas, A. R. (1990). *Security of title in Canadian water rights.* Calgary, Canada: Canadian Institute of Resources Law.

Milly, P. C. D., Betancourt, J., Falkenmark, M., Hirsch, R. M., Kundzewicz, Z. W., Lettenmaier, D. P., & Stouffer, R. J. (2008). Stationarity is dead: Whither water management? *Science, New Series, 319*, 573–574.

Moore, M., Shaw, K., & Castleden, H. (2018). 'We need more data!' The politics of scientific information for water governance in the context of hydraulic fracturing. *Water Alternatives, 11*(1), 142–162.

Moore, M., von der Porten, S., & Castleden, H. (2017). Consultation is not consent: Hydraulic fracturing and water governance on indigenous lands in Canada. *Wiley Interdisciplinary Reviews, 4.* np-n/a. doi:10.1002/wat2.1180

Neuman, J. C. (2004). The good, the bad, and the ugly: The first ten years of the Oregon water trust. *Nebraska Law Review, 83*, 432.

Nowlan, L. (2005). *Buried treasure: Groundwater permitting and pricing in Canada.* Toronto: Walter and Duncan Gordon Foundation.

Nowlan, L. (2012). CPR for Canadian rivers: Law to protect and conserve environmental flows in Canada. *Journal of Environmental Law and Practice, 23*(3), 237–286.

Ontario Water Resources Act, RSO 1990, c O.40.

Pahl-Wostl, C., Sendzimir, J., Jeffrey, P., Aerts, J., Berkamp, G., & Cross, K. (2007). Managing change toward adaptive water management through social learning. *Ecology and Society, 12*, 30.

Passelac-Ross, M., & Buss, K. (2011). Water stewardship in the lower Athabasca river: Is the Alberta government paying attention to aboriginal rights to water? *Journal of Environmental Law and Practice, 23*, 69–83.

Percy, D. R. (1988). *The framework of water rights legislation in Canada.* Calgary: Canadian Institute of Resources Law.

Percy, D. R. (2004). The limits of Western Canadian water allocation law. *Journal of Environmental Law and Practice, 14*, 315.

Phare, M.-A. (2009). *Denying the source: The crisis of first nations water rights.* Victoria, Canada: Rocky Mountain Books.

Rose, C. (1990). Energy and efficiency in the realignment of common-law water rights. *The Journal of Legal Studies, 19*, 261–296.

Ruhl, J. B. (1997). Thinking of environmental law as a complex adaptive system: How to clean up the environment by making a mess of environmental law. *Houston Law Review, 34*, 933.

Ruhl, J. B. (2010). Climate change adaptation and the structural transformation of environmental law. *Environmental Law, 40*, 363–431.

Sabatier, P. A., Focht, W., Lubell, M., Trachtenberg, Z., Veditz, A., & Matlock, M. (eds). (2005). *Swimming upstream: Collaborative approaches to watershed management*. Cambridge, Massachusetts: The MIT Press.

Sandford, R. W. (2017). *Our vanishing glaciers: The Snows of yesteryear and the future climate of the Mountain West*. Victoria, Canada: Rocky Mountain Books.

Sinclair, A., Doelle, M., & Duinker, P. (2017). Looking up, down, and sideways: Preconceiving cumulative effects assessment as a mindset. *Environmental Impact Assessment Review, 62*, 183–194.

Sprague, J. B. (2007). Great wet North? Canada's myth of water abundance. In K. Bakker (Ed.), *Eau Canada: The future of Canada's water* (pp. 23–36). Vancouver, Canada: UBC Press.

The upper Nicola band of the Okanagan (Syilx) nation and the lower Nicola, coldwater, Nooaitch and Shackan bands of the Nlaka'pamux nation, as represented by their chiefs and councils and her majesty the queen in right of the province of British Columbia, as represented by the minister of indigenous relations and reconciliation. Nicola Watershed Pilot Memorandum of Understanding. 2018.

The Water Rights Act, no date CCSM, c W80, s 2.

The Water Security Agency Act, SS 2005, c W-8.1.

Unger, J. (2009). *Consistency and accountability in implementing watershed plans in Alberta: A jurisdictional review and recommendations for reform*. Edmonton: Environmental Law Centre.

Walters, C. J., & Holling, C. S. (1990). Large-scale management experiments and learning by doing. *Ecology, 71*(6), 2060.

Water Act, RSA 2000, c W-3, s 5.

Water Act, SPEI 2017, c 17.

Water Resources Act, SNL 2002, c W-4.01.

Water Resources Protection Act see *An Act to affirm the collective nature of water resources and provide for increased water resource protection*.

Water Sustainability Act, SBC 2014, c 15, s 5.

Watercourse and Wetland Alteration Regulation – Clean Water Act, New Brunswick Regulation 90-80, OC 90-532, 1990.

Watercourse and Wetland Protection Regulations, EC720/08.

Wittwer, G. (2011). Confusing policy and catastrophe: Buybacks and drought in the Murray–Darling Basin. *Economic Papers, 30*(3), 289–295.

Proof of sufficient water resources as a prerequisite for the authorization of new urban developments: the Spanish model

Roberto O. Bustillo Bolado and Laura Movilla Pateiro

Introduction

The goal of this Commentary is to introduce Spanish legal developments regarding the effect of water resources on urban planning over the last few decades. As a consequence of these developments, it is now mandatory that the competent public authorities report on the existence of sufficient water resources to fulfil projected needs from the anticipated urban developments (new residential areas, industrial zones, etc.).

For decades Spain suffered from unsustainable economic growth based on the building industry and property speculation. That unsustainable economic growth, together with climate change, led to the overexploitation of surface and groundwater and resulted in insufficient water supply in some geographic areas.

Consequently, in 1999 the legislature introduced a requirement for the competent territorial authority to report on the existence of sufficient water resources during the elaboration of the urban plans. Data and information provided by engineers and other scientists affiliated with the State Public Administration are an essential part of those reports. Since then, a combination of legislative will – although with poor legislative technique – and evolving judicial criteria have been gradually reinforcing the requirement to produce a report proving adequate water resources, and now submission of these reports is mandatory and binding.

Conclusions in this article have been deduced from the analysis of pertinent legislation (2001 Water Act, 2008 Soil Act, and Additional Provision 2.4 of the 13/2003 Public Works Act), case law (several court decisions resolving conflicts in several Spanish basins, especially in the Mediterranean area), and legal-scientific doctrine. An understanding of the Spanish experience, its legislative and judicial evolution and its difficulties may be helpful for other states. This study is therefore meant to contribute to the balance between urban planning and the rational use of water resources in the context of sustainable development.

Origin and legal evolution of the report on the existence of sufficient water resources

The 1978 Spanish Constitution (adopted at the end of the Franco dictatorship and still in force) has been referred as 'the begetter of the most fruitful and creative period for Spanish Water Law' (Embid Irujo, 2003, p. 290). The legal and political model established by this constitutional text required a new act superseding the centenary 1879 Water Act and its numerous reforms and complementary legal texts. In this sense, the preamble of the new 1985 Water Act explained how the old 1879 Water Act was not able to respond to the requirements of the new territorial organization of the state. The preamble also stated that the new act should take into account the new decentralized organization and create a framework of cooperation among all the public administrations to achieve rational and adequate protection of water resources.

Article 149.1.22ª of the Spanish Constitution reserved to the state the regulation, planning and licensing of water resources and water uses when the water resources flow between two or more Spanish autonomous communities.[1] That reservation to the state resulted in significant consequences and complexities regarding the allocation of jurisdictional competence over water. First, jurisdiction over water resources was divided between the state and the autonomous communities. The state has competence on any basin shared by two or more autonomous communities – through transboundary basin bodies called *confederaciones hidrográficas* – and an autonomous community has authority over the basins entirely within its territory. Second, the system of distribution of competencies designed by the 1978 constitution gave rise to shared competency between the state, autonomous communities and local authorities over the territory of basins shared by two or more autonomous communities. Together with the general responsibility of the state for those basins addressed in Article 149.1.22ª, the autonomous communities have jurisdiction in various related fields (territorial planning, urban planning and housing, public works of interest to the autonomous community, forests and forest uses, etc. – Articles 148.1.3, 148.1.4, 148.1.8), and there are also competencies assigned to local authorities by virtue of the autonomy granted by the constitution (Article 140).

Therefore, one of the main challenges of the 1999 legislation was to create mechanisms to reconcile the jurisdiction of the states with that of the autonomous communities and the local authorities in this field.

In some respects, Act 46/1999 (modifying the 1985 Water Act) reinforced some of the provisions of the 1985 Water Act. The fourth paragraph added to the current Article 25 of the 1985 Water Act (also modified by the final disposition of Act 11/2005 (which modified the 2001 act related to the National Hydrologic Plan) states that the confederaciones hidrograficas must issue a preliminary report regarding uses and regulation of water resources in the planning carried out by the Spanish autonomous communities. This article itself seems to leave no doubt regarding the mandatory nature of the report on the existence of sufficient water resources, although there is no language stating that the report is binding on the decision-makers. However, during the last few years, numerous rulings of the Spanish High Court have introduced and reinforced the binding character of the report by also considering the application of other two legal dispositions to concession contracts for public works: Article 15.3 of the 2008 Soil Act and paragraph 4 of the Second Additional Disposition to Act 13/2003.[2]

Article 15.3 of the 2008 Soil Act establishes the need to obtain a report on the existence of sufficient water resources to satisfy new demands and on the protection of the public water domain; the report must be obtained from the administration in charge of water resources. Plus, the report on water resources will be decisive for the content of the environmental report, which may only differ from it in an expressly justified way. For its part, the Second Additional Disposition to Act 13/2003 high-lights the binding force of the report on water resources. On numerous occasions, the parties whose plans have been blocked by the report have looked to the courts for relief, and their arguments have been soundly rejected by the Spanish High Court (Decisions of 24 April 2012, 25 September 2012, 14 November 2014, and 17 June 2015, among others).

Case law requirements of the report

Today there is abundant and mostly consistent case law from the third chamber of the Spanish High Court regarding the reports issued by the confederaciones hidrográficas.[3] The court decisions refer to urban and territorial planning instruments according to the mentioned Article 25 of the 1985 Water Act, Article 15.3 of the 2008 Soil Act, and paragraph 4 of the Second Additional Disposition to the Public Works Act (13/2003). Here is a summary of the main points of this case law.

- *Regarding the character of the report.*

(1) The report is mandatory in any case, with no need to prove an impact of the plan on water use. It is for the confederación hidrográfica concerned to consider the impact (decision of the Spanish High Court of 15 July 2015).
(2) The report is binding with regard to the scope of competencies of the confed-eraciones hidrográficas, whose mandate is to ensure sufficient water resources and protection of the public water domain. There is nothing to prevent a confederación hidrográfica from making a statement on other related legal issues, but the report will not be binding with respect to those aspects. From this perspective, the *binding* character of the report stated in paragraph 4 of the Second Additional Disposition to Act 13/2003 matches the *decisive* character of the report established by the 2008 Soil Act (decisions of the High Court of 14 November 2014 and 20 July 2015, in which the court ruled that the decisive character of the report gave it a binding force).
(3) The final adoption of a legal instrument adopting or implementing urban or territorial planning without that report or against its binding content will be null (decisions of the High Court of 19 December 2013, 20 July 2015, 2 September 2015, 11 February 2016 and 30 November 2016, among others).

- *Regarding the content of the report.*

(1) The report must analyze the use and availability of the water resources, including both physical (e.g., sufficiency) and legal aspects (e.g. legal limits to the use of water). The contributions of qualified technical staff (scientists and engineers) are

of crucial importance in the analysis and evaluation of the water resources (decisions of the High Court of 18 March 2014, 14 November 2014 or 17 June 2015).

(2) It is not only the future existence of adequate water resources that matters. It is even more important that sufficiency of the resource is guaranteed at the moment of the adoption of the planning. That is to say, for instance, that if there is not enough water at present, a favourable report cannot be given, even if the plan includes the actions needed to obtain those resources in the future (decisions of the High Court of 10 April 2014, 11 June 2015, and 12 June 2015, among others). Obviously, a favourable report cannot be given if those future actions have been declared null by a final judgement (decision of the High Court of 8 November 2016).

(3) To be favourable, the report needs to be precise and clear. Ambiguities and inaccuracies are not admissible. The sufficiency of water resources must be directly ensured, or at least that the planned actions do not imply an increase in water demand (decisions of the High Court of 12 June 2015 and 17 July 2015, among others).

- *Regarding the legislation of the autonomous communities.*

(1) Within the field of competence of the state – transboundary basins shared by two or more autonomous communities – the regional legislation cannot replace the report by the confederaciones hidrográficas with the report of other public or private bodies – since 2009 there is a change from the previous case law (decisions of the High Court of 14 November 2014 and of 17 June 2015).

(2) Within the field of competence of the autonomous communities – basins entirely within the territory of one autonomous community – the High Court has understood that a report from the public water administration concerned is also needed. The legislation of each autonomous community will determine the specific competent regional body. However, the autonomous community cannot eliminate the requirement for the report or render it meaningless (decision of the High Court of 12 July 2015). Although this case law has a positive effect on the protection of water resources, in our opinion, the need for the report from the public water administration concerned should be expressly enshrined in binding legal regulations (Pallarés Serrano, 2015, pp. 503–505).

- *Regarding interim administrative judicial protection.*

(1) If an instrument of urban or territorial planning that does not have a favourable report from the confederación hidrográfica is involved in a contentious matter in the administrative courts, a provisional measure that suspends the enforceability of the contested planning measure may be adopted (decisions of the High Court of 25 February 2009, 1 February 2010, 9 February 2010, and 11 November 2011).

The influence of sustainable development as an implicit constitutional principle

The expression 'sustainable development' (Bustillo Bolado & Gómez Manresa, 2014) does not appear in the text of the Spanish Constitution, whose original drafting preceded by almost a decade the introduction of the term in the 1987 Brundtland Report, *Our Common Future* (World Commission on Environment and Development, 1987). However, almost immediately, case law linked this concept to the constitution by taking the content of Articles 45 (environment and quality of life) and 130 (development of the public sector) as a reference.[4] This interpretation of the constitution also coincides in time with a general rise of environmental awareness in the debate over resource exploitation in Spain (Leandro Del Moral, van der Werff, Bakker, & Handmer, 2003).

The first and most relevant step in this regard was taken with the Constitutional Court's Decision 102/1995, which states the following, regarding environment as a sphere of competence (translation by the authors):

> The configuration of competence in this matter, shared by the state and the autonomous communities, contains a static and objective element: the environment as such. It also contains a dynamic and functional element: the protection of the environment. Both aspects of such public activity raise an environmental dimension of other sectoral policies.... In short, there is a right of everyone to enjoy the environment and a duty of conservation that weighs on everyone, plus a mandate to the public authorities on its protection (Article 45 of the Spanish Constitution). The indicated connection becomes explicit when the public powers are entrusted with the function of promoting and developing all economic sectors, and thus, improving the standard of living, with a direct reference to certain resources (agriculture, livestock, fisheries) and some natural spaces (mountain areas) (Article 130 of the Spanish Constitution), which has led us to highlight the need to harmonize development with the environment (Constitutional Court Decision 64/1982). This is, in other words, 'sustainable development', a balanced and rational development that does not forget future generations, highlighted in 1987 in what is known as the Brundtland Report, with the title *Our Common Future,* commissioned by the General Assembly of the United Nations.

Shortly after, the Third Chamber of the Supreme Court, in the fourth legal basis of its decision of 30 May 1997, and again in the legal basis of its judgement of 31 March 1998, included in its *ratio decidendi* invocations of sustainable development as a requirement derived from Article 45 of the Spanish Constitution. In the same line, more recently, we can point to the fourth legal basis of the decision 1512/2008, of October 8, of the High Court of Justice of the Autonomous Community of Valencia, as well as the legal basis of the High Court of Justice of the Autonomous Community of Andalusia (Seville) of 7 March 2006.

Thus, it can be argued that sustainable development – a concept that was born and interpreted in the framework of the United Nations System (Söderbaum & Tortajada, 2011) and that has been promoted by national laws and European law – has been adopted by Spanish case law, not only as a legal concept or principle, but as a *constitutional* principle under Article 45 of the Spanish Constitution. Therefore, without being expressly enshrined in the Spanish Constitution, the principle has been understood as clearly deducible from its articles.

This interpretation of the principle of sustainable development by the Spanish courts has important repercussions for the purposes of this study. Through Articles 9.1 and 53.3 of the Spanish Constitution and 5.1 of the Organic Law of the Judiciary, sustainable development, as an implicit constitutional principle, should be taken into account by judicial bodies when interpreting and applying laws and regulations, even if the court deals with regulatory areas in whose positive texts no express reference is made to this legal concept.

This consideration of sustainable development as an implicit constitutional principle is a clear endorsement in Spain that legal norms and interpretations must present an adequate and necessary reconciliation between the desire for economic growth and the need to conserve the environment and natural resources. Rejection of new urban developments that are not preceded by a favourable report of water sufficiency proves the embrace of this balance.

As explained clearly by Judge Carlos Altarriba Cano in his dissenting opinion on the decision of the Chamber of Administrative Litigation of the High Court of Justice of the Autonomous Community of Valencia of 8 July 2010 (translation by the authors):

> What is evident is that, following the Directive [the judge refers to the 2000 Water Framework Directive of the European Union], the existence of sufficient water resources constitutes a prerequisite of any territorial planning act.... Water resources are not a normative element of the plan. They are a planning element prior to the plan; likewise the landscape, orography, soil, atmosphere, forests, or surface waters. Water resources are an absolutely indispensable element, without which any act of the administrative procedure aimed at approval of a plan is impossible. I can deduce that from paragraph 2 of Article 45 of our Constitution ... ; or from Article 47.... In this way, if there are not enough water resources ... the administrative act that intends to implement a plan in these conditions is irrational, unmotivated, disproportionate, and arbitrary.

Static or dynamic control?

As mentioned, in accordance with the Spanish legislation in force, any new urban planning instrument needs to prove that there is enough water to cover the new planned uses, as a prerequisite to its approval. However, is that requirement exhausted only before the approval of the plan, or is it a continuous requirement that remains in effect throughout the life of the plan? In other words, is the requirement of water sufficiency a static or a dynamic requirement?

In principle, it is a static requirement. The existence of sufficient water resources is only verified prior to the approval of the plan. At first glance, this appears as a deficiency of the system. But it is partly overcome due to the dynamics of the Spanish urban planning model, in which the General Plan of each municipality – which is subject to this static requirement – must be completed or supplemented later by other more detailed instruments, whose approval is also subject to the requirement for water sufficiency.

An adequate understanding of this statement requires a brief explanation of the essential aspects of the Spanish urban planning model. It is very important to take into account that since the Constitutional Court's Decision 61/1997 of 20 March, legislating on urban planning is considered an exclusive competence of each of the 17 autonomous communities. However, the autonomous systems are faithful to a Spanish tradition which started from the urban planning model foreseen in the prior (state) act of 12 May 1956 – today superseded by the 2008 Soil Act – which was excellent, modern and forward-looking. For this reason, although formally there are 17 systems for urban planning, in the essential aspects they follow a single model, described hereinafter (Martín Rebollo and Bustillo Bolado, 2009).

The most important urban planning instrument in each municipality is the General Plan. This instrument extends its regulatory effects throughout the entire municipal territory. However, this does not mean that it affects that whole space equally. The precision and detail of the plan's regulations are asymmetric. For some areas of the territory, the General Plan will be so detailed that it may not need any subsequent normative complement; this is the case usually in already urbanized and built-up spaces for which no substantial changes are foreseen. However, in areas that are going to experience important alterations, the content of the General Plan will necessarily be inaccurate and sparsely detailed. In these cases, the plan limits itself to fixing the guidelines of the forthcoming planning; the remaining details will need to be provided by future instruments, such as partial plans or urban action programmes.

Let us imagine, for instance, that in 2019 a Spanish municipality submits to the respective confederación hidrográfica a draft General Plan for evaluation. The only substantial change foreseen in the territory is the creation of an industrial park on five hectares of land that, at the time of the elaboration of the project, is an area of unprotected mountain pastures. The General Plan is completely detailed in what affects the rest of the municipality, but regarding a substantial change to this area it only establishes general guidelines. The details are left for a later time and a partial plan that affects only those five hectares. Let us also imagine that there is an aquifer whose resources are considered sufficient to supply the projected needs of the future industrial park. This justifies a favourable report for the General Plan in 2017, after which it is immediately approved, published and enters into force. In 2022, a private entity is interested in developing this industrial area, so together with the City Council it promotes a partial plan for later execution. The partial plan is submitted to the respective confenderación hidrográfica for evaluation. However, compared to 2017, the situation has changed substantially, because in 2020 a severe seismic movement affected the aquifer, significantly reducing its capacity. This change justifies and requires that the confederación hidrográfica issue an unfavourable report in 2022, which pre-vents the draft partial plan from being approved. Does this mean that the disposition in the General Plan regarding the expected five-hectare industrial park has been repealed? It does not. It is still in force; it has not been repealed. However, as long as there is not enough water (and, in this example, in 2020, there is not), the complementary planning instrument (the partial plan) that would be needed to realize the provisions of the General Plan will not be legally possible. In such conditions, the municipality has two options. The first is to wait for a miracle (or a hydraulic work) that supplies the water necessary to sustain those five desired hectares of industrial land. The second option is to modify its General Plan by reducing or eliminating those foreseen industrial uses, thereby adapting the plan to its new water reality.

Consequently, the monitoring of the sufficiency of water resources made by the report of the confederacion hidrográfica is, in principle, static. However, the sequential model of Spanish urban planning allows certain dynamic effects that enable adaptation to changing water circumstances.

In any case, even when the exposed indirect dynamic effect of the report may not be deployed – for example, because the projected urban developments are described in great detail in the General Plan, which is unlikely but not impossible in legal terms – there would be a final possibility of control: the submission of each concrete project to environmental assessment according to the legally foreseen terms (on this issue, among others, see (state) Act 21/2013 of 9 December, on environmental assessment).

Responding to an unfavourable report

What are the legal means available for stakeholders to respond to a report by a confederación hidrográfica that might be detrimental to their interests? In the first place, it should be highlighted that if a local or regional competent public administration approves an urban or territorial planning measure that goes against the report, this decision will be null. Regardless of the argument used by the competent public administration, the report is binding. That is to say, this form of reaction – though frequently used by the autonomous communities – must absolutely be discarded as illegal and would be easily declared as such by the competent court.

Second, and also on the basis of the binding force of the report, a non-favourable report serves as a decision on the merits, and the plan will not be approved. Spanish administrative procedural regulations (Article 112.1 of Act 39/2015, on the common administrative procedures of the Public Administrations, and Article 25 of Act 29/1998, regulating contentious administrative regulations) allow parties to directly contest the report in court. Conversely, even if the report is favourable, it does not determine the outcome of the case on the merits. The plan might be not approved due to other circumstances that bear no relation to the report. In this case, the only mechanism for redress in the Spanish legal system is to contest the legality of the resolution that approved the plan itself, by claiming that the report is deficient.

Concluding remarks

The following main conclusions can be drawn from the analysis made in this study.

1. Today no urban plan can be lawfully passed in Spain without an official report that proves the existence of sufficient water resources.

2. Qualified technical staff (scientists and engineers) must participate with legal staff in the elaboration of these reports.

3. The case law of the Third Chamber of the Supreme Court is consistent regarding the mandatory and binding nature of the reports issued by the conferederaciones hidrográficas on the sufficiency of water resources and the protection of the public water domain, and the reports must be obtained in conjunction with approval, modification or review of instruments of territorial and urban planning. Logically, plans adopted in the absence of or contrary to the reports are void.

4. The report on the sufficiency of water resources implies, in the terms described in this paper, static control over urban planning instruments. Nevertheless, there are legal

means that prevent the implementation of a plan when, after its approval, the water situation that justified the favourable report change or disappear. In this way the Spanish system indirectly provides for dynamic control.

5. Without prejudice to the fact that some of the foundations of the examined case law can be disputed – especially as regards their projection to the intra-community basins, whose legal regime should depend on the decision of the legislators from the autonomous communities – we understand that such case law, which considers water an essential and increasingly scarce natural resource, favours the satisfaction of the principle of sustainable development. Consideration of sustainable development as a constitutional principle is mandatory for judicial bodies (Article 9 of the Spanish Constitution and Article 5.1 of Organic Law 6/1985 of the Judiciary).

6. A combination of several factors is needed to try to prevent violation of legal protection of water resources:

- Social awareness and education on sustainable development
- Public authorities objectively serving the general interest and providing a high level of technical preparation through highly skilled engineers and scientists who can transmit that knowledge to other people (e.g. judges) lacking technical knowledge
- Independent judicial bodies taking into account the constitutional principle of sustainable development when interpreting and applying the law
- Citizen access to judicial processes
- Clear and precise legislation.

7. Ultimately, the evolution of Spanish positive law and its judicial interpretation should be valued very positively regarding its effects. Thanks to these reports on water sufficiency and their consideration as mandatory and binding, the Spanish legal system has effective tools to invalidate many undesirable urban plans, especially on the Mediterranean coasts. These annulled urban plans represented a model of urban planning based on speculative growth and were contrary to the basic idea that no newly constructed uses can be allowed where there is not enough water to satisfy their needs.

Notes

1. Since the 1978 constitution, the Spanish state is formed by 17 autonomous communities (with autonomy in certain legal and political senses) and two autonomous cities.
2. The High Court is the highest judicial instance in Spain. The decisions of inferior courts can be appealed in cassation before it. Its rulings need to be taken into account by the inferior courts when carrying out their judicial functions.
3. If there are two or more decisions of one chamber of the High Court interpreting the law in a specific way, the inferior Spanish courts need to also interpret the law in that way. However, if the inferior tribunals appreciate new concurrent reasons, they can deviate from the decisions of the High Court in a motivated manner.
4. The two first paragraphs of Article 45 SC state: '1. Everyone has the right to enjoy an environment suitable for personal development, as well as the duty to preserve it. 2. The

public authorities shall safeguard rational use of all natural resources with a view to protecting and improving the quality of life and preserving and restoring the environment, by relying on essential collective solidarity.' The first paragraph of Article 130 SC states: '1. The public authorities shall attend to the modernization and development of all economic sectors and, in particular, those of agriculture, livestock raising, fishing and handcrafts, to bring the standard of living of all Spaniards up to the same level.'

Disclosure statement

No potential conflict of interest was reported by the authors.

References

Bustillo Bolado, R. O., & Gómez Manresa, M. F. (2014). *Desarrollo sostenible análisis jurisprudencial y de políticas públicas*. Navarra: Aranzadi.

Embid Irujo, A. (2003). Water Law in Spain After 1985. *Water International, 28*(3), 290–294.

Leandro Del Moral, L., van der Werff, P., Bakker, K., & Handmer, J. (2003). Global trends and water policy in Spain. *Water International, 28*(3), 358–366.

Martín Rebollo, L., & Bustillo Bolado, R., (Coords.). (2009). *Fundamentos de Derecho Urbanístico* (Vol. 2, 2ª ed.). Navarra: Aranzadi.

Pallarés Serrano, A. (2015). La coordinación de los planes que ordenan el medio físico: El papel de la Planificación Hidrológica. In A. Embid Irujo (Ed.), *El segundo ciclo de Planificación Hidrológica en España (2010-2014)* (pp. 477–509). Navarra: Aranzadi.

Söderbaum, P., & Tortajada, C. (2011). Perspectives for water management within the context of sustainable development. *Water International, 36*(7), 812–827.

World Commission on Environment and Development. (1987). *Our common future*. Oxford: Oxford University Press.

Understanding water disputes in Chile with text and data mining tools

Mauricio Herrera, Cristian Candia, Diego Rivera, Douglas Aitken, Daniel Brieba, Camila Boettiger, Guillermo Donoso and Alex Godoy-Faúndez

ABSTRACT

This article provides a multidimensional study based on data and text mining of prosecuted disputes on water rights in Chile, and an analysis of the state's capacity, particularly of the institutions related to water regulation. This study shows not only a substantial increase of legal disputes regarding water rights over the years (1981–2014), but also clear patterns in the geographic location of these conflicts, as well as in the types of legal actions, arguments and strategies used in their pursuit. Through a topic analysis, we find a growing diversification over time of the subjects contained in the legal claims, suggesting an increase in structure and complexity.

Introduction

The Chilean water market and the legal framework around water rights: a brief contextualization

The Chilean system of water management and allocation is an interesting case study due to its unusual tradable water rights system (Bauer, 2015). Few other places, such as some of the western states of the United States, South Africa, Australia, Iran and Spain's Canary Islands, also have water trading schemes (Saleth & Dinar, 2005). This system has attracted considerable analysis by proponents and critics because of its strongly free-market approach, reducing to a minimum the interference of the state as the main actor to drive water allocation (Bauer, 2005, 2015; Budds, 2004, 2009; Hearne & Donoso, 2014; Vergara, 2002, 2015).

Since 1981 the water market framework in Chile has been dictated by the Chilean Water Code. The Chilean Water Code regulates water allocation as a de facto private property right separated from land, freely traded and subject to minimal state regulation, even though water resources are defined as a national good for public use under the Chilean Constitution (Section 19, paragraph 23; see also Section 595 of the Civil Code and Section 5 of the Water Code). Under the Water Code, the Chilean state grants a petitioner's rights for the use of surface water and groundwater. Once all water rights have been allocated within a basin, the management of water rights at the watershed scale is overseen by water users' organizations (WUOs). These entities are supposed to manage the shared resources from the same river, channel, aquifer or reservoir and act as decentralized private organizations independent of the state (Retamal et al., 2012; Vergara, 2015).

A state agency, the General Water Directorate (Dirección General de Aguas, DGA), is mandated to protect the resource and maintain an updated nation-wide inventory of water resources, as well as a registry of granted water rights. Thus, the Chilean state is legislator, regulator and surveyor of water resources and should provide updated and reliable information regarding water uses and management. The state also has a role in settling water rights conflicts, both through the DGA and through the judiciary branch of the Republic of Chile, including the Supreme Court and the Courts of Appeal.

The overall legal framework thus seeks to foster water markets as a secondary allocation mechanism among users with no direct governmental intervention. The primary allocation depends on a nonmarket system under governmental management. If there is available water within a basin or watershed after governmental intervention, it can be reallocated through the exchange of water rights, i.e., the right to use certain amounts of water, either for a limited time (lease) or in perpetuity (sale).

Some economists argue that water trading can promote more efficient water distribution because theoretically a market-based price acts as an incentive for users to reallocate resources from low-value activities to high-value activities. In practice, however, water markets have also created distortions, such as frequent stockpiling of water rights, where users hold water rights without using them, for speculative purposes (Scott, 1995). Difficulties in correctly assessing the social and environmental outcomes of water trading schemes, and the ethics of applying economic principles to a resource such as water, have raised concerns regarding the fairness of water markets in secondary allocation (Donoso, 2011).

The Water Code reform

In 2005, the Water Code was significantly amended. The main concerns this reform sought to address were the insufficiency of state regulation to ensure effective functioning of water markets, and, relatedly, the need to discourage the stockpiling of water rights (Hearne & Donoso, 2005). The reform sought to reduce possible monopolistic distortion in the water and energy markets and to mitigate the effect of unused water rights on the economic development of the basins (Bauer, 2015). To achieve these goals, the reform established a fee applicable to unused surface and groundwater rights, to reduce hoarding. The reform also introduced tools for improving the management of aquifers and for expanding the powers of administrative evaluation concerning requests of water rights. For instance, it allowed the DGA to deny entirely or in part a water right petition if the volume requested was not justified by its proposed use (Article 147 *bis* of the Water Code), thus matching the authorized use of the resource to the amount of water actually required. Finally, the reform allowed users to solve disputes in local courts, instead of having to litigate in a single court in the capital (Santiago), facilitating their access to the judicial system. In these ways, structural changes were made to water legislation in 2005 with the intent of enhancing sustainability, efficiency and equity in the use of this resource.

Sources of conflicts and new approaches to understanding them

Chile's economy, particularly in the agricultural and mining sectors, is greatly dependent on reliable freshwater resources. Agriculture is the dominant consumer by a considerable margin; the demand for water by the agricultural sector is estimated at 82% of total use, according to the DGA Water Atlas 2016. In the years 2010 to 2016, Chile's central and central-northern (Norte Chico) zones were hit by a 'mega drought', which has been linked to a combination of climate change and natural variability (Boisier, Rondanelli, Garreaud, & Muñoz, 2016; Garreaud et al., 2017). This phenomenon affected over 60% of the agricultural industry's export products. The mining industry also suffered, particularly in the region of Antofagasta, where the industry is the largest water consumer (Aitken, Rivera, Godoy-Faúndez, & Holzapfel, 2016). Due to the demands of the mining and industrial sectors, many of Chile's regions are under considerable hydric stress due to low water availability, variability in supply and the increasing impact of climate change (OECD, 2015). Water scarcity increases the costs of copper production (which amounts to 13% of GDP), due to higher consumption of desalinated water (water–energy trade-off). It also lowers farm productivity because of higher crop losses and lower crop yields. These effects increase food prices, destroy jobs and increase operational costs for both mining and agriculture companies. This situation puts a substantial proportion of Chile's economy at considerable risk and must be addressed accordingly.

Aitken et al. (2016) showed that all of Chile's central-north and northern regions currently have water stress indices greater than 1 (high overexploitation), with a value as high as 51.6 for the region of Antofagasta (the main mining region), once environmental flow demands were considered. In most regions, agriculture accounted for around 70–90% of water demand. In Antofagasta, however, mining was calculated to account for about 64% of total water demand. This situation in which demand in specific sectors far exceeds water availability has a potential for severe conflict.

The unequal distribution of water rights, coupled with increasingly unbalanced water budgets, is generating tension among water users amidst more intense competition for this resource. Thus, rising water demand and climate/geographical variability create conflicts both between water right holders and between them and local communities, who often feel powerless due to their lack of financial resources to press their claims. These conflicts involving water rights holders need to be resolved within a WUO, whether or not the holders share the same water source (Hearne & Donoso, 2014; World Bank, 2013). Water users can now appeal decisions of the WUO to ordinary courts. Therefore, when legal disputes occur between parties, it is the ultimate responsibility of the courts to settle the conflict. According to the Water Code, there are several institutions (e.g., WUOs, DGA, Courts of Appeal, Supreme Court) with diverse degrees of authority who are empowered to render decisions on water uses.

In terms of the country's overall governance framework for water issues, the World Bank (2011, 2013) finds that the complexity of the current institutional framework often leads to duplication in the execution of functions, gaps of omission, and problems of coordination between different agencies and organizations. There are also several institutional problems linked to low levels of funding, an inefficient system for generating relevant information, poor definition of policies and sectorial objectives, and the lack of institutional coordination. Thus, uncoordinated actions among these institutions, not based on reliable data, could produce inefficiencies and diminish the state's capacity to resolve conflicts.

However, perceptions about water conflict resolution have so far been mostly based on fragmentary evidence (Bauer, 2015) or on users' and academics' opinions (Vergara, 2015). For instance, water users' perceptions of institutional capacity to solve conflicts are mainly based on their experiences. Thus, users may conclude that institutions are making subjective judgements and that rules are being bent or broken depending on litigants' relative (and highly asymmetrical) economic power.

In an attempt to go beyond perceptions and understand regional variations in water conflicts through data, Rivera et al. (2016) used a new approach based on geotagging of the public legal records of judiciary judgments, as a proxy for the geographical distribution of conflicts. They found that the number of water conflicts varies regionally, which yielded spatial patterns correlated with economic activities and the availability of water resources. For example, in northern regions, conflicts over water rights usually occur between agricultural and mining operations. In Chile's more densely populated central zone, conflicts are mostly related to the ownership of water rights, both between farmers and the water authority (DGA), and between farmers seeking water for irrigation use and companies in charge of the drinking water supply.

These results, however, concern the general pattern of water-related conflicts and do not consider the details, evolution or complexity of the conflicts, the relationship between conflicts and increasing demand of water among different sectors, or the impacts of climate change and of successive regulatory reforms. Therefore, further analysis is needed to address these unanswered questions. Concretely, how have legal demands – which are viewed as a proxy for conflict – evolved due to the increasing tension between industrial, agricultural and drinking water supply sectors arising from climate change and the unequal distribution of water rights? What was the real impact of regulatory reforms in the water rights market? How effective is the state in solving water-related conflicts?

Legal records as a tool for the spatial-temporal characterization of conflicts related to water

The 1981 Water Code is based on a strong role of the judiciary as arbitrator in resolving disputes and enforcing management decisions. Therefore, one of the best ways to bridge science and policy, and to support the decision-making process in water-related issues, could be to analyze all available legal texts and data, using data mining tools (Sunil, 2013, 2014).

We propose a multidimensional study based on data and text mining of disputes (Waltl, Matthes, Waltl, & Grass, 2016) involving water rights conflicts brought before the courts, together with an analysis of the capacity of the state's institutions to manage these conflicts. These cases can be used as a proxy for water-related conflicts and therefore to analyze the dynamics and content of these conflicts for a better understanding of typical actions, resources and fundamentals of the claims in water rights lawsuits. This approach can also provide results based on data analysis to confirm or reject perceptions among water users regarding these issues.

Material, methods and exploratory data analysis

Data sources for this study: water stakeholders and legal actions

This work is based on historical case study research dating back to 1981, for which we analyzed almost 4000 legal demands (public legal records) made by stakeholders and water users. All these records are judgments and decisions issued by the Supreme Court (in Santiago, the capital city) and by Courts of Appeal, which are regional courts located in the major cities of the country. These data are available at the judiciary system website (http://www.pjud.cl) and were compiled by an external entity (Microjuris, 2017). For clarity, in this study, we considered the regions (the largest political-administrative divisions) of Chile as territorial units for the analysis. We also used records of registered water rights (DGA, 2017a) and records from the Public Registry of User Organizations reported by the General Water Directorate on their website (DGA, 2017b), as well as DGA personnel data (from http://transparencia.dga.cl/).

Computer-assisted analysis of jurisprudence

Generally, legal action is the result of an unresolved conflict that has escalated due to failure of the parties to reach an agreed resolution in a first instance. Therefore, lawsuits can be taken as a proxy for an underlying conflict. Thus, we used legal actions as proxies to understand the dynamics, complexity, diversity and content of these conflicts (Wyner, Mochales-Palau, Moens, & Milward, 2010). This work differs from Rivera et al. (2016) in that it uses text mining techniques to analyze discourses instead of merely registering the occurrence of conflicts.

Using text mining tools, we extracted information from water lawsuit documents such as the Water Code's sections, regulations, and codes used by lawyers and judges in legal proceedings. We call this procedure computer-assisted analysis of jurisprudence. The *feature extraction algorithm* identifies articles related to the water code, the mining code, the civil code and civil procedure that appeared in the text of pleadings filed in the lawsuit procedures, as well as the final verdict, which is used as a label to classify the result as failed/rejected or successful/not rejected. With this information we build *vectors of features*, which are used to search for patterns by data mining techniques.

The number and diversity of legal concepts in the lawsuit procedures registered in the vectors of features were used to discover the different legal strategies, the types of actions and the fundamental arguments of the claims in each ruled case. With the computer-assisted analysis of jurisprudence we found that most water right legal procedures can be put under several major themes related to the protection of property and the environment, property regularization, and legal formalism, in agreement with other studies (Hearne & Donoso, 2014; Rivera et al., 2016).

Topic modelling

To better understand the nature of these conflicts, we applied topic modelling techniques from text mining to legal texts (Firdhous, 2010). Topic modelling is a type of statistical modelling used to discover the latent topics in a corpus or collection of documents. We used it as a procedure for deriving high-quality information from the analyzed texts to understand in greater detail the issues covered by water-related legal demands over time (Merkl & Schweighofer, 1997). This kind of analysis allows us to delve into the context and local reality of each region, including inferring the causes that ultimately lead to legal action.

Using the texts of almost 4000 legal rulings provided by the Microjuris database (Microjuris.com, 2017), we constructed a corpus, and from this corpus we extracted 'hidden variables' or subjects. With the help of some probabilistic topic models (Steyvers & Griths, 2007), such as the latent Dirichlet allocation (LDA) model, we uncovered the thematic structure of the corpus built from the documents of the judicial proceedings.

The LDA model (Blei & Lafferty, 2009) assumes that each document in a corpus contains a mix of topics. However, the topic structure is hidden (or 'latent') because we can only observe the documents and words, not the topics themselves. This method infers the topic structure from the known words and documents.

For LDA, it is necessary to specify in advance the number of topics in the underlying topic structure. We used perplexity (Berthard, Ghosh, Martin, & Summer, 2009) to determine the optimal number of themes. Perplexity is a statistical measure of how well a probability model predicts a sample. As applied to LDA, for a given value of the number of topics, the parameters for the LDA model are estimated. Then, given the theoretical word distributions represented by the topics, the result is compared to the actual theme mixtures, or the distribution of words in the documents. This statistic is somewhat meaningless on its own. The benefit comes from comparing perplexity across different models with varying numbers of topics. The model with the lowest perplexity is generally considered the best.

Once we defined the number of topics, we analyzed the complete corpus built from all the available documents, from 1981 to 2014, to infer the structure of topics covered by all legal claims. After that, for a more detailed analysis – to understand the context of legal demands, and the contents and causes that lead to the most frequent type of legal actions – we split the corpus into three parts to balance them according to the number of conflicts. The 1980s and 1990s provided a significantly smaller number of documents per year. Therefore, to have a statistically significant sample for topic modelling, we included all documents up to the year 2000 in our first period of analysis. Specifically, we separated the corpus into three time intervals: $t_1 = 1981$–2000, $t_2 = 2001$–2008 and $t_3 = 2009$–2014.

For each set of documents in each period, we chose an optimal number k of topics according to the lowest perplexity criterion and used LDA to identify the topic representation in each document and the words associated with each topic. For this, we used Gibbs sampling (Casella & George, 1992). A basic summary of this algorithm is as follows:

(1) The algorithm runs through each document in the corpus, and randomly assigns each word in the document to one of k topics. This random assignment already provides both topic representations of all the documents and word distributions of all the topics. But because it's random, this is not yet a very accurate structure.

(2) To improve it, for each document d, the algorithm goes through each word w in d and for each topic t computes

  • the proportion of words in document d that are currently assigned to topic t, i. e., the conditional probability $p(t|d)$; and

  • the proportion of assignments to topic t over all documents that come from this word w, $p(w|t)$.

  • It then reassigns w to a new topic, where the topic t is chosen with probability $p(t|d) \times p(w|t)$. This is the probability that topic t generated word w. In other words, in this step, we are assuming that all topic assignments except for the current word in question are correct, so the assignment of the topic by adding the newest word is updated. After repeating the previous step many times, the algorithm eventually reaches a roughly steady state, where the assignments could be considered good.

(3) Using these assignments, it is possible to estimate

  • the topic mixture of each document (by counting the proportion of words assigned to each topic within that document); and

  • the words associated with each topic (by counting the proportion of words assigned to each topic overall).

In what follows, the analysis proceeds in two steps. First, through an exploratory data analysis, we show some major patterns and trends in the granting of water rights and in judicial rulings over time. We connect these trends with the state's ability to mediate conflict through administrative and judicial channels, as well as with the apparent effects of the 2005 reform to the Water Code. In the second step, we proceed to the topic modelling.

Results

First screening of data on the structure of the Chilean system of water management and allocation

A first screening of data showed that Chile has more than 3000 WUOs across the country, 50 Surveillance River Boards, and nearly 200 Associations for Water Channels (canal users). These stakeholder organizations related to water distribution and consumption create a complex system of interrelationships.

In addition to these organizations, there are state agencies responsible for granting water use rights, regulating the market and developing infrastructures for water use.

Figure 1 shows the number of water-use rights granted by the DGA throughout the country. Figures 1(a,b) are choropleth maps of Chile for regions and communes, respectively, with darkening shades representing a greater number of water rights granted by the DGA, the state agency in charge of this process. Chile has a high diversity of ecosystems, leading to four climatic regions. From Figure 1(a), it is apparent

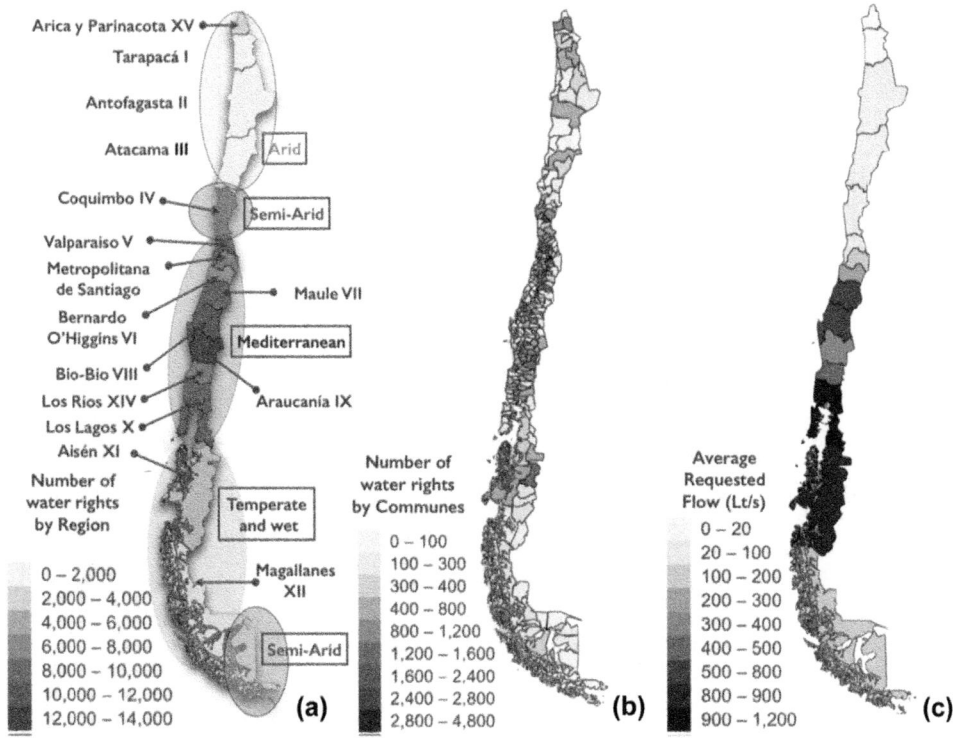

Figure 1. (a) Chile's administrative regions and climatic zones (labelled in boxes). Darker shades indicate a greater number of water use rights that have been granted by the General Water Directorate. (b) Water rights distribution by commune within each region. The requests for water rights are accompanied by demands for flows. (c) Average flow requested in each region, with darker shades indicating greater requested flows.

that the number of granted water rights correlates with water availability in different climatic regions. This is not a coincidence. There is little availability of water in the north, so the number of water rights is also low, while the central zone has a more humid climate, with more water, and therefore more water rights for trading.

More water rights granted, despite the Water Code reform

The 2005 Water Code reform introduced tools to improve the management of aquifers and to expand the powers of administrative evaluation concerning requests for water rights, matching the use of the resource with the amount of water required. Because the reform strengthened regulatory authority over future grants of water use rights by establishing additional requirements for the petition of new rights, fewer grants of water rights might have been expected. Moreover, in 2005 Chile began to be affected by a severe drought, which caused a significantly less availability of water resources. In this sense, our results (Figure 2) are counterintuitive.

The main chart in that figure shows the evolution in the number of judicial rulings, while the inset shows the number of water rights granted over time. After the 2005 amendment to the Water Code there was a significant *increase* in the number of newly

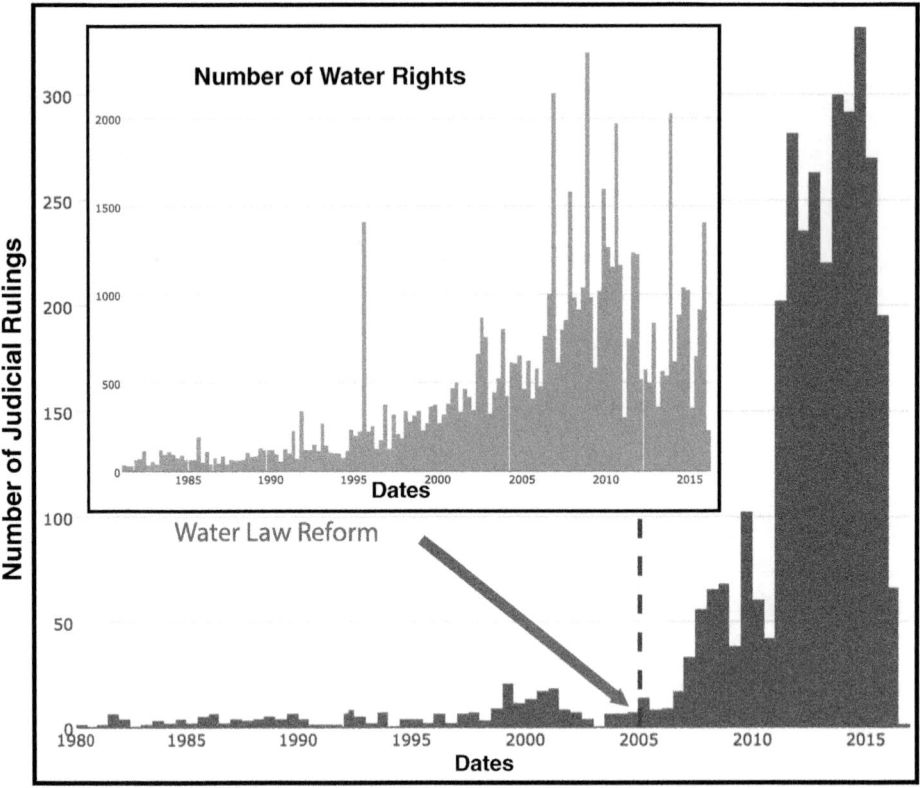

Figure 2. Larger panel: evolution of legal demands over time (DGA, 2017a). Inset panel: evolution in number of water rights over time.

granted water rights in practically all regions of the country. Two additional patterns are also apparent: the 'explosion' of legal claims after the modification of the Water Code in 2005; and the correlation (with some delay) between the granting of water rights and the explosion in legal disputes.

Water Code reform and real water demand

What might have caused this almost simultaneous explosion in the allocation of water rights and in legal disputes? The granting of new water rights has been accompanied by an increase in market demand for more water. Figure 3 shows the average flow requested by users in each region. In this figure, if we compare the requested flow associated with the water rights market with the demand for water calculated from information from specialized government agencies, we can see that in all regions the water rights market demand for flow (Market) is significantly higher than the demand for flow reported by government agencies (Demand). In other words, allocated water rights systematically exceed physical water flows actually consumed by users. Therefore, we can formulate at least two, mutually non-exclusive hypotheses: water supply calculations made by government agencies are not correct; and users ask for, and get, more

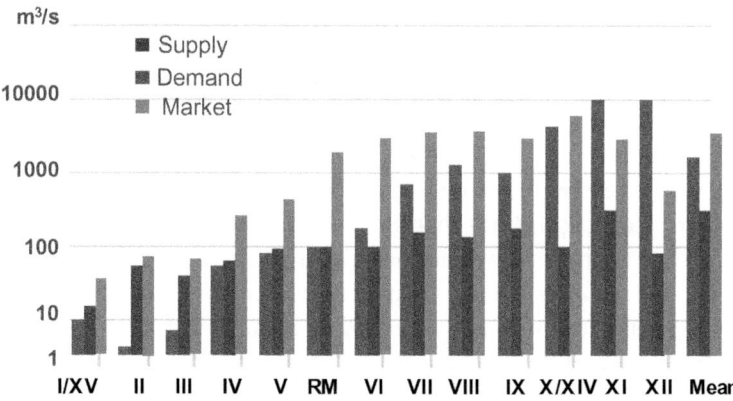

Figure 3. Water supply and demand in 2010, by region. Adapted from World Bank (2011).

water rights than they need, and therefore the market for water rights contains a high degree of speculation.

If the first hypothesis is true, one possible explanation is that governmental agencies miscalculated the water supply, because the official data were provided by the last water balance from 1987, itself based on records taken between 1951 and 1980. Those data, for example, did not include climate change and variability impacts, such as the high decadal variability of rainfall amounts (Montecinos & Aceituno, 2003; Quintana & Aceituno, 2012; Valdés-Pineda et al., 2014). Thus, they over-allocated water rights because they overestimated the available hydric resources.

If we assume the second hypothesis to be dominant, we conclude that the state agency in charge of regulating the market has failed to match the granting of new water rights to actual demand, thus encouraging market speculation in water rights. This is a powerful stimulus for conflict under conditions of water scarcity.

Water Code reform and non-local resolution of conflicts

One important achievement of the reform was introducing the possibility for stakeholders to resolve conflicts through the local civil courts, giving more users access to justice. Indeed, as we saw above, our results confirm an increase in the number of lawsuits in local civil courts, which suggests the reform has worked in the intended direction.

But the inefficiency of the system is also evident from the analysis of the data. Our exploratory data analysis shows that more than 25% of legal claims end up in the Appeals and Supreme courts, which are both extremely centralized and outside the local framework supposedly favoured by the code. For instance, as shown by Rivera et al. (2016), most appeals are settled in a single court located in Santiago, where the DGA is, regardless of the location of the conflict. This is due to a double judicial review system, in which the decisions of the Courts of Appeal can finally be decided by the Supreme Court if the dissatisfied party appeals (appeal of cassation). Thus, the losing party can always appeal the decision of the regional court to the Supreme Court. This could overload the judicial system in the long run. Indeed, and inasmuch as cases 'travel upwards' to regional courts and then to Santiago, the final resolution of conflicts through local courts – as intended by the Water Code reform – has not been achieved. This non-local resolution of conflicts suggests excessive centralization of the current institutional framework, which is paradoxical for water markets considered as a tool for decentralized conflict resolution.

According to the Water Code, many legal claims must be directly filed against the DGA. In our study, nearly 50% of registered litigations were conducted in this manner. Our exploratory data analysis finds that the DGA has lost up to 73% of these cases. This is highly suggestive of the low capacity of state organizations (Fukuyama, 2013), in the sense of having low technical and/or financial resources to execute its tasks adequately. Indeed, the DGA may lose so many cases either because its initial grant (or denial) of water rights to consumers was technically or legally deficient – forcing users to appeal to the courts for rectification – or because, having made reasonable allocations in the first place, its legal capabilities are so weak that the DGA can easily be defeated by users (particularly those with considerable legal support) in the courts.

Indeed, and notwithstanding the plausibility of the first possibility just discussed, the water authority's legal resources seem highly unequal to their task. A review of the DGA's personnel – publicly accessible thanks to transparency laws – reveals that in a typical month (June 2015), 39 lawyers were working at the DGA (data from http://transparencia.dga.cl/). Only 27 of the 39 lawyers were hired on a permanent or semi-permanent basis (as opposed to fee-for-services schemes), and only they can represent the DGA in court. Moreover, only 10 of the permanent or semi-permanent lawyers had functions which plausibly included representing the DGA in court, and only two of them had job descriptions which specified 'litigation' as their main occupation. Considering the several hundreds of outstanding legal cases at any one time, these figures seem low. Moreover, of these 10 possible litigation lawyers, 9 were employed in Santiago, which suggests that the water authority's capacity to litigate effectively at the local and regional levels may be particularly weak. Most lawyers are, in any case, assigned to the legal tasks associated with the allocation of water rights. Finally, if the DGA must resort to the ordinary courts of justice to request compliance with the sanctions they imposed and file complaints with the courts for infractions such as illegal extractions, the increased number of lawsuits could well overwhelm the DGA's capacity to resolve these cases.

Furthermore, the current legal and administrative framework provides important limitations on the DGA that prevent it from carrying out its work effectively. For example, the DGA must resort to the ordinary courts of justice to request compliance with the imposed sanctions; it must appeal to the Public Ministry, like any other individual; and it must eventually request the legal support of the State Defence Council (Consejo de Defensa del Estado) to register complaints with the courts on illegal extractions. Also, to add to the litany of weaknesses, the DGA does not have guaranteed access to the groundwater wells to carry out its enforcement function (World Bank, 2013). Of course, this is how the Water Code was initially constructed, relying on a strong role of the judiciary, with administrative agencies controlled at the end by the judges as arbitrators for resolving disputes.

Understanding legal complexities using topic modelling

Using 3827 legal text documents (legal rulings) provided by the Microjuris database (Microjuris, 2017), we build one complete corpus for our topic analysis. We estimated the optimal number of topics in the corpus by using the perplexity criterion and obtained more than 40 topics for the entire corpus.

Figure 4 shows the results of the topic analysis using the LDA model (Jurafsky & Martin, 2000). In Figure 4(a) the density graph shows an increase over time in the number and diversity of topics treated in the analyzed legal texts, which in turn suggests an increase in the number, diversity and complexity of underlying conflicts. Figure 4(b) shows the thematic structure of the corpus. Topics are numbered for easy viewing and are represented by nodes in a network, with sizes proportional to the frequency of each topic's occurrence over time. The links represent the interrelation between topics, and the 'clouds' around the set of nodes, with different colours,[1] separate the communities, that is, clusters with common global legal themes.

Topic analysis provides rich information that allows us to understand different sources of conflicts and at the same time to look for plausible explanations of the nature of these conflicts. In turn, this could help suggest proposals for future legal reforms. For example, one of the most frequent topics is Topic 1, represented by a large node in the upper central part of Figure 4(b). This topic is *groundwater use*. As mentioned, the DGA does not have guaranteed access to groundwater wells for their control (World Bank, 2013). On the other hand, with an extreme drought underway, the search for new sources of water is critical, so many conflicts can be expected given this combination of factors. This fact could be considered in future reforms of DGA responsibilities.

Topic 17 is another frequent topic, *cassation resources*. A cassation resource is an extraordinary resource with the purpose of nullifying a judicial sentence that contains an incorrect interpretation or application. The decisions of the regional courts may eventually be modified by the Supreme Court if the dissatisfied party interposes a cassation resource. The frequent occurrence of this specific topic is a confirmation that many claims end up, first, in the regional Appeals courts, and then in the Supreme Court. Both instances are centralized and outside the local framework of conflict

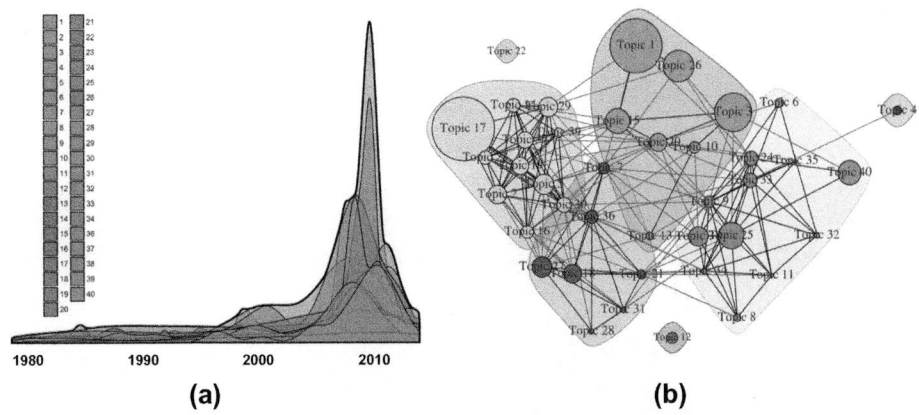

(a)   **(b)**

Figure 4. Topic modelling using latent Dirichlet allocation of a corpus formed from 3827 documents of legal rulings provided by the Microjuris database (Microjuris.com, 2017). (a) Density graph for 40 topics treated in legal text through time. Topics are numbered and represented with different colours. (b) Community structures for the network of topics. The size of the network nodes is related to the frequency with which the topic appears. Seven communities are shown.

resolution intended by the reform of the Water Code. In turn, *Topic 3* addresses issues of property protection and regularization. If we continued making new analyses in this way, we could uncover the detailed structure of underlying conflicts related to water use in the entire corpus.

We also performed a more detailed analysis of the data through a time segmentation of the corpus. The main goal was to reduce the number of topics in the analyzed corpus, to understand, as in the previous analysis, the context, contents and causes of frequent legal actions, while at the same time capturing some variations (dynamics) in the structure of conflict over time. For this, we split the corpus into three time intervals: t_1 = 1981–2000, t_2 = 2001–2008 and t_3 = 2009–2014. With this segmentation, we have balanced samples of the corpus for each time interval. Of course, other segmentations are possible. For example, it may be useful to split the data (the corpus) according to periods with relevant Chilean historical, social, administrative or climatic events to study their effects on conflicts. However, for the purpose of demonstrating variances over time in the structure of the corpus and hence capturing some dynamic aspects of the underlying structures of conflict, we believe it is sufficient to consider the proposed data partition.

For each set of documents in each period, we chose an optimal number k of topics according to the lowest perplexity criterion and used an LDA model for topic modelling. Since the lowest calculated perplexity score was obtained for 15 topics in all periods (t_1, t_2 and t_3), the LDA model (Grüen & Hornik, 2011) was set to produce that number of topics. After running the code, the outputs showed diversification over time of the topics in legal claims (Figures 5–7), suggesting a certain increase in the complexity of conflicts over time. Although the optimal *number* of topics (calculated using the perplexity criterion) stays about the same (15), the subjects are mostly different in each period, and they are interconnected in different

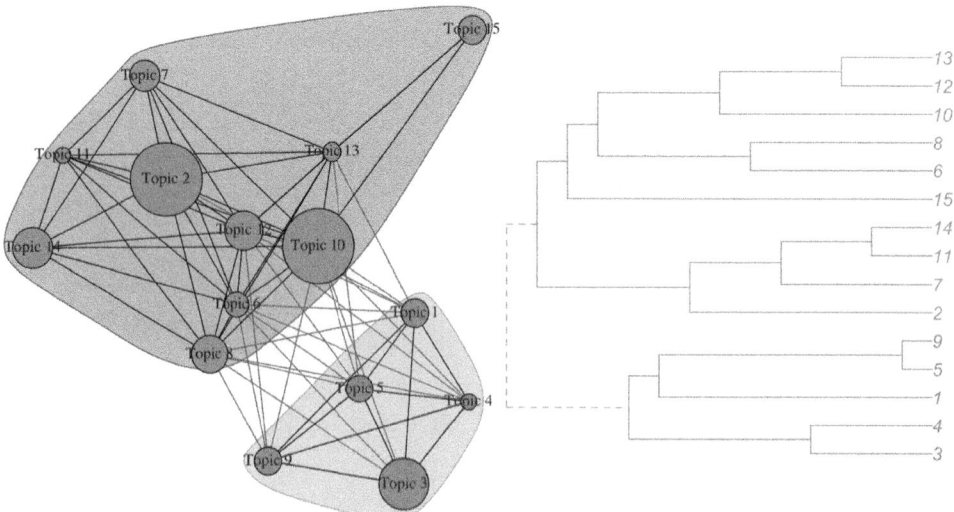

Figure 5. Community structure, 1980–2000. The communities and their topics are Protection of Property and the Environment (2, 6, 7, 8, 10, 11, 12, 13, 14, 15) and Claims and Property Regularization (1, 3, 4, 5, 9).

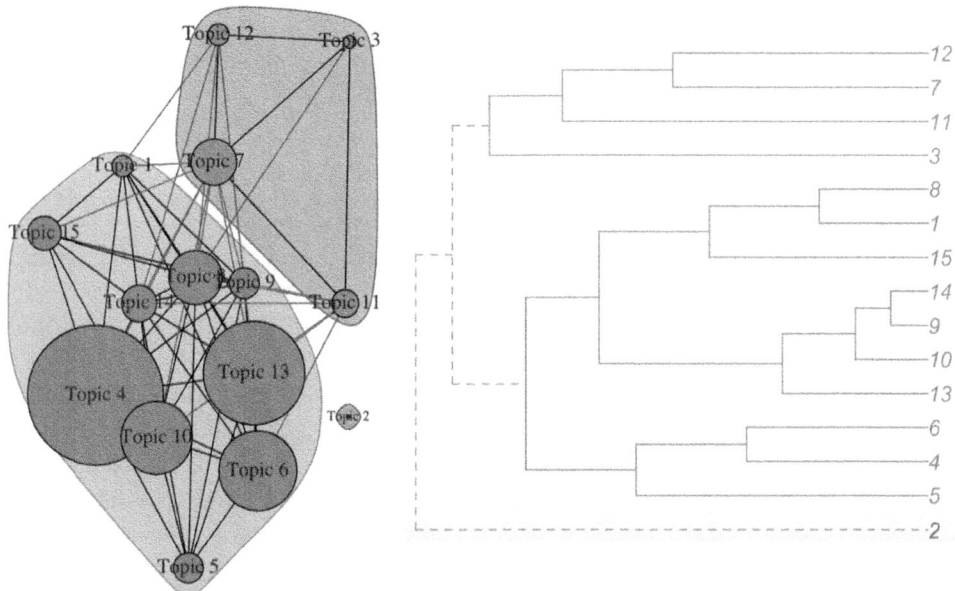

Figure 6. Community structure, 2001–2008. The communities and their topics are Protection of Property and the Environment (3, 7, 11, 12); Claims and Property Regularization (1, 4, 5, 6, 8, 9, 10, 13, 14, 15); and Bidding, Companies, Competition and Market (2).

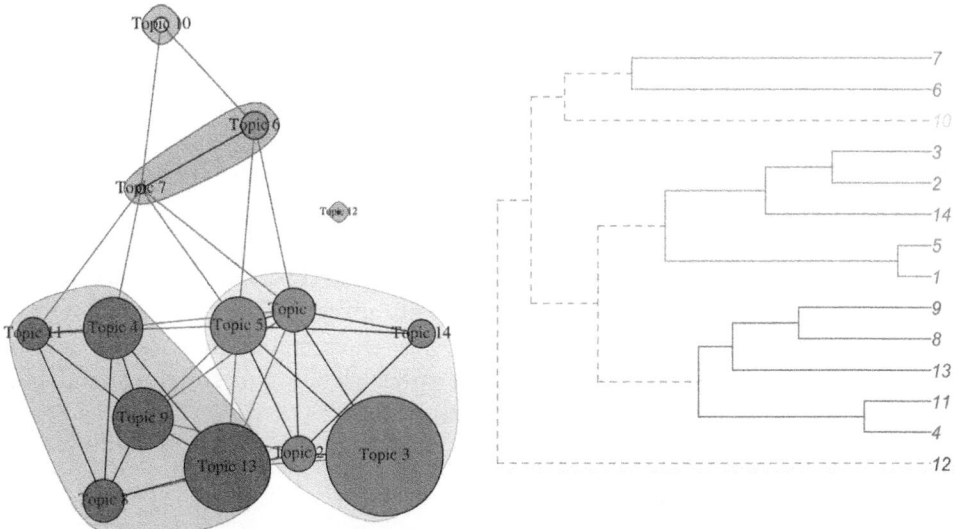

Figure 7. Community structure, 2009–2014. The communities and their topics are Relationship with Companies (6, 7); Bidding, Companies, Competition and Market (10); Protection of property and the environment (1, 2, 3, 5, 14). Claims and Property Regularization (4, 8, 9, 11, 13); and Formalism, Individual, Judicial Process (12).

ways over time. The topic interconnections were measured by the number of common keywords shared by the topics.

Understanding legal complexities by community structure of topics

Network analysis

To build the network of word distributions across topics (topic interaction), we used the subjects, found by the LDA model, as network nodes and the common keywords between these topics as proxies for network edges between the nodes. Topic modelling enables the detection of the most frequent subjects per period and thus the most recurrent sources of conflict. In this network representation, the radius of the node is proportional to the frequency of appearance of the corresponding topic at any given period. For example, in 1981–2000 (Figure 5), groundwater was not an issue. Instead, problems related to protection of property and the environment were the major causes of conflict. On the other hand, in 2001–2008 (Figure 6), topics 4 and 13, related to the regularization of property, stand out as important causes of conflict. Finally, in 2009–2014 (Figure 7), topic 3, related to groundwater claims (as in the previous analysis for the entire corpus), acquired a clear relevance, represented by a larger node in the network. This period was marked by serious water scarcity in different regions of the country, which in turn eventually produced an overexploitation of groundwater.

Community structure of topics

The goal of community detection is to find the 'natural lines' along which a network separates, that is, the division of the nodes of a network into groups, clusters or communities according to the pattern of edges in the network. The number and size of the groups into which the network is divided are not specified by the domain specialist; they are determined by the network itself and computed by a community detection algorithm (Newman, 2006).

The identified communities correspond to the more common types of actions and fundamentals of the legal claims. The community detection algorithm appears to have picked out the global structure of water-conflict-related topics and their interrelationships using the analysis of network data alone. Moreover, this community structure for the network of topics evolves over time, tending to diversify among several dominant topics per cluster or network group. Further, new emerging communities with fewer links between them appear, suggesting more specialization and structure (and thus, greater complexity) in the types of legal demands.

Discussion and conclusions

Market-focused approaches tend to overlook that water is a crucial resource for local communities and in many cases also has cultural meaning and helps shape collective identity. As a result, and particularly under conditions of growing scarcity, a water allocation framework based on market transactions is likely to be a source of considerable conflict. In fact, as public opinion and users' and academics' views suggest (Bauer, 2015, Vergara, 2015), the current diagnosis is of an ongoing and growing number of water-related conflicts throughout the country, while the institutional capacity to resolve them remains weak. In this work, we have provided results based on data and text mining that confirm this shared perception.

The 1981 Chilean Water Code granted a strong role for the judiciary as an arbitrator of water rights disputes and in securing compliance with water management decisions. We therefore used available judicial decisions to assess the real magnitude and dynamics of water-related conflicts. Our results show an explosion of legal claims, particularly after the 2005 Water Code reform. One interpretation of this fact is that the modification of the Water Code was not the immediate catalyst of the rapid growth in lawsuits. Rather, by easing access to justice, the modification of the code 'opened the door' to reveal a number of important conflicts that were hidden behind the apparent economic benefits of the free market for water and which also arose due to climate drivers and increasing competition for this scarce resource. At the same time, some strong indicators of poor regulation of the market and powerful incentives for conflict emerged from our data analysis. For example, the state agency in charge of regulating the market, the DGA, granted so many new water rights that the rights have exceeded real demand, prompting market speculation.

Furthermore, the DGA has lost up to 73% of the legal cases in which it has been involved. This is highly suggestive of a state organization with inadequate technical and/or financial capacities to competently assign water rights and defend the state's interests in court. Furthermore, our results confirmed the excessive centralization of the institutional framework in dealing with water-related conflicts. This may be a sign of the lack of capacity of local courts to resolve local conflicts, which risks overloading the judicial system in the long run. This situation is at odds with the inspiring idea behind water markets, which considers as a basic and desirable principle the minimizing of state intervention.

In this work we adopted a new approach, through network analysis and topic modelling, to understand common types of actions, legal resources and the fundamentals of claims in water rights lawsuits. Considering court judgments as proxies for underlying water-related conflicts and using topic modelling, we found the most frequent subjects that represented the most typical sources of conflicts through time. For example, in 1981–2000, problems related to protection of property and the environment were major causes of conflicts; in 2001–2008, regularization of property (i.e., water rights) stands out as an important cause of disputes; and in 2009–2014, over-exploitation of groundwater due to surface water scarcity and poor DGA control of groundwater wells were the most frequent cause of conflicts.

Our results for the community structure of the network of topics showed an overall map of conflicts through these three periods. Some overall patterns were clearly revealed, such as the evolution to fewer but more frequent (dominant) topics per cluster/network group, new emerging network groups, and fewer but stronger links between community members, revealing an increase in complexity. These observations allow us to capture the evolution and global trends of underlying conflicts related to the use of water.

In 2018 a new reform of the Water Code was proposed by the current government. The reform intends to change the structure of perpetual water rights to a type of temporary and administrative use permit, and to give stronger powers to the DGA to limit the exercise of water rights for environmental reasons (Celume, 2015). We believe that this is a great opportunity for a more critical appreciation of the complexities involved in water resources regulation and processes of development. One way to accomplish this goal is by bridging science and public policy through data sciences and by taking the necessary actions and reforms to solve the real issues that generate conflicts.

Note

1. Readers of the print version can view the figures in colour in the online article at https://doi.org/10.1080/02508060.2019.1599774

Acknowledgements

We acknowledge the Commission for Scientific & Technological Research (CONICYT) for supporting our research funded by the Fifth National Competition for Research Centers in Priority Areas CONICYT/FONDAP/15130015; and CONICYT/FONDECYT/ Postdoctorado-3150558

Disclosure statement

No potential conflict of interest was reported by the authors.

Funding

This work was supported by the Fifth National Competition for Research Centers in Priority Areas of National Commission for Scientific & Technological Research CONICYT/FONDAP/15130015; and CONICYT/FONDECYT/ Postdoctorado-3150558.

References

Aitken, D., Rivera, D., Godoy-Faúndez, A., & Holzapfel, E. (2016). Water scarcity and the impact of the mining and agricultural sectors in Chile. *Sustainability, 8*(2), 128.

Bauer, C. J. (2005). In the image of the market: The Chilean model of water resources management. *International Journal of Water, 3*(2), 146–165.

Bauer, C. J. (2015). Water conflicts and entrenched governance problems in Chile's market model. *Water Alternatives, 8*(2), 147–172.

Berthard, S., Ghosh, S., Martin, J. H., & Summer, T. (2009). Topic model methods for automatically identifying out-of-scope resources. In *JCDL '09: Proceedings of the 9th ACM/IEEE-CS Joint Conference on Digital Libraries,* 6, 19–28. New York, NY: ACM.

Blei, D., & Lafferty, J. (2009). Topic models. In A. Srivastava & M. Sahami (Eds.), *Text mining: Classification, clustering, and applications chapman & hall/CRC data mining and knowledge discovery series* (pp. 71–89). Boca Raton, FL.

Boisier, J. P., Rondanelli, R., Garreaud, R. D., & Muñoz, F. (2016). Anthropogenic and natural contributions to the Southeast Pacific precipitation decline and recent megadrought in central Chile. *Geophysical Research Letters, 43*(1), 413–421.

Budds, J. (2004). Power, nature and neoliberalism: The political ecology of water in Chile. *Singapore Journal of Tropical Geography, 25*(3), 322–342.

Budds, J. (2009). Contested H2O: Science, policy and politics in water resources management in Chile. *Geoforum, 40*(3), 418–430.

Casella, G., & George, E. I. (1992). Explaining the Gibbs Sampler. *The American Statistician, 46*(3), 167.

Celume, T. (2015). Pilares sobre los que se sustenta la reforma al Código de Aguas chileno y desafíos pendientes. *Actas de Derecho de Aguas, 5,* 39–50.

DGA. (2017a). *Derechos de aprovechamiento de aguas registrados en DGA*. Retrieved from http://www.dga.cl/productosyservicios/derechos_historicos/Paginas/default.aspx

DGA. (2017b). *Registro Público de Organizaciones de Usuarios*. Retrieved from http://www.dga.cl/administracionrecursoshidricos/OU/Paginas/default.aspx

Donoso, G. (2011). *WP6 IBE EX-POST case studies*. The Chilean water allocation mechanism, established in its Water Code of 1981. Deliverable No. D6.1 – IBE Review Reports. Lessons learned. Prepared under contract from the European Commission Grant Agreement No. 265213 FP7 Environment. Deliverable no.: D6.1 – IBE Review Reports Lessons learned. Retrieved from http://www.feem-project.net/epiwater/docs/d32-d6-1/CS30_Chile.pdf

Firdhous, M. F. M. (2010). Automating legal research through data mining. *International Journal of Advanced Computer Science and Applications - IJACSA, 1*(6), 9–16.

Fukuyama, F. (2013). What is governance? *Governance, 26*(3), 347–3686.

Garreaud, R. D., Alvarez-Garreton, C., Barichivich, J., Boisier, J. P., Christie, D., Galleguillos, M., & Zambrano-Bigiarini, M. (2017). The 2010–2015 megadrought in central Chile: Impacts on regional hydroclimate and vegetation. *Hydrology and Earth System Sciences, 21*(12), 6307–6327.

Grüen, B., & Hornik, K. (2011). Topic models: An R package for fitting topic models. *Journal of Statistical Software, 40*(13), 1–30.

Hearne, R., & Donoso, G. (2005). Water institutional reforms in Chile. *Water Policy, 7*(1), 53–69.

Hearne, R., & Donoso, G. (2014). Water markets in Chile: Are they meeting needs?. In W. Easter & Q. Qiuqiong (Eds.), *Water markets for the 21st century: What have we learned?* (Vol. 11, pp. 103–126). Springer.

Jurafsky, D., & Martin, J. (2000). *Speech and language processing: An introduction to natural language processing, computational linguistics, and speech recognition* (2nd ed.). Engle-wood Cliffs, NJ: Prentice Hall.

Merkl, D., & Schweighofer, E. (1997). En route to data. Mining in legal text corpora: Clustering, Neural. Computation, and international treaties. Proceedings of the 8º International Workshopond Database and Expert Systems Aplications. Toulouse, 465–470.

Microjuris.com, (2017) *Access to database*. Retrieved from http://cl.microjuris.com/home.jsp

Montecinos, A., & Aceituno, P. (2003). Seasonality of the ENSO-related rainfall variability in central Chile and associated circulation anomalies. *Journal of Climate, 16*(2), 281–296.

Newman, M. E. J. (2006). Modularity and community structure in networks. *Proceedings of the National Academy of Sciences, 103*, 8577–8582.

OECD. (2015). *Water resources allocation: Sharing risks and opportunities, OECD studies on water*. Paris: Author. doi:10.1787/9789264229631-en

Quintana, J. M., & Aceituno, P. (2012). *Changes in the rainfall regime along the extratropical west coast of South America (Chile): 30-43º S. Atmósfera, 25*(1), 1-22. Retrieved 10 April 2019, from http://www.scielo.org.mx/scielo.php?script=sci_arttext&pid=S0187-62362012000100001&lng=es&tlng=en

Retamal, R., Melo, O., & Arumi, J. L., & Parra, Ó. (2012). Sustainable water governance: From a sectoral management system to an integrated one? In D. Rivera (Ed.). *Chile: Environmental, political and social issues* (pp 33–68). Hauppage, NY: Nova Science

Rivera, D., Godoy-Faúndez, A., Lillo, M., Alvez, A., Delgado, V., Gonzalo-Martín, C., & García-Pedrero, Á. (2016). Legal disputes as a proxy for regional conflicts over water rights in Chile. *Journal of Hydrology, 535*, 36–45.

Saleth, R. M., & Dinar, A. (2005). Water institutional reforms: Theory and practice. *Water Policy, 7*, 1–19.

Scott, W. R. (1995). *Institutions and organizations*. Thousand Oaks, CA: SAGE.

Steyvers, M., & Griths, T. (2007). Probabilistic topic models. *Handbook of Latent Semantic Analysis, 427*(7), 424–440.

Sunil, R. (2013). Knowledge discovery from legal documents dataset using text mining techniques. *International Journal of Computer Applications, 66*(23), 32–34.

Sunil, R. (2014). Exploratory analysis of legal documents using unsupervised text mining techniques. *International Journal of Engineering Research & Technology, 3*(2), 2264–2267.

Valdés-Pineda, R., Pizarro, R., García-Chevesich, P., Valdés, J. B., Olivares, C., Vera, M., …
Helwig, B. (2014). Water governance in Chile: Availability, management and climate change.
Journal of Hydrology, 519, 2538–2567.

Vergara, A. (2002). Las aguas como bien público (no estatal) y lo privado en el derecho chileno:
Evolución legislativa y su proyecto de reforma. *Revista de Derecho Administrativo Económico,
IV*(1), 63–79.

Vergara, A. (2015). *Crisis institucional del agua. Descripción del modelo, crítica a la burocracia y
propuesta de tribunales especiales* (2ª ed.). Santiago: Thomson Reuters, Ediciones UC.

Waltl, B., Matthes, F., Waltl, T., & Grass, T. (2016). *LEXIA - A data science environment for
semantic analysis of German legal texts, IRIS: Internationales rechtsinformatik symposium.*
Salzburg, Austria.

World Bank. (2011). *Diagnóstico de la gestión de los recursos hídricos.* Departamento de Medio
Ambiente y Desarrollo Sostenible Region para América Latina y el Caribe, CHILE. Retrieved
from http://www.dga.cl/eventos/Diagnostico%20gestion%20de%20recursos%20hidricos%20en
%20Chile_Banco%20Mundial.pdf

World Bank. (2013). *Estudio para el mejoramiento del marco institucional para la gestión del
agua.* Departamento de Medio Ambiente y Desarrollo Sostenible Region para América Latina
y el Caribe, CHILE. Retrieved from http://reformacodigodeaguas.carey.cl/wp-content/uploads/
2014/09/Informe-Banco-Mundial-Estudio-para-el-mejoramiento-del-marco-institucional.pdf

Wyner, A., Mochales-Palau, R., Moens, M. F., & Milward, D. (2010). Approaches to text mining
arguments from legal cases. In E. Francesconi, S. Montemagni, W. Peters, & D. Tiscornia
(Eds.), *Semantic processing of legal texts. Lecture notes in computer science* (Vol. 6036, pp. 60–
79). Berlin, Heidelberg: Springer.

Bringing back ecological flows: migratory fish, hydropower and legal maladaptivity in the governance of Finnish rivers

Niko Soininen, Antti Belinskij, Anssi Vainikka and Hannu Huuskonen

ABSTRACT

Historically, Finnish rivers supported vital populations of migratory salmonids. Presently, these species are more or less endangered due to extensive damming and hydropower production. In this article, we study the main legal and scientific drivers for re-evaluating some of the existing hydropower operations in Finland. We argue that there is a need for re-evaluation on the basis of legal obligations stemming largely from EU law and new scientific knowledge. Theoretically, our setting opens up a classical adaptive governance problem in how to address laws and past decisions that are based on outdated assumptions about the functioning of social-ecological systems.

Introduction

Prior to the industrial revolution, Finland boasted 25 Atlantic salmon (*Salmo salar*, hereafter salmon) and some 72 anadromous brown trout (*Salmo trutta*, hereafter trout) rivers running to the Baltic Sea, four rivers supporting both species (Teno, Näätämö, Paatsjoki, Tuulomajoki) with outlets to the Barents Sea (HELCOM, 2011a), and two inland rivers with reproducing landlocked Atlantic salmon populations. Currently, the number of Finnish rivers sustaining natural reproduction of salmon has been reduced to four, and only small and rare populations of wild anadromous brown trout, migratory whitefish and migratory grayling have survived in rivers with a connection to the Baltic Sea (HELCOM, 2011a). In Finland, the anadromous brown trout and landlocked Atlantic salmon are classified as critically endangered, the freshwater brown trout as endangered, and the anadromous Atlantic salmon as vulnerable (Rassi, Hyvärinen, Juslén, & Mannerkoski, 2010).

The near-complete loss of spawning habitats for migratory salmonids resulted primarily from the large-scale damming of rivers for hydropower production (HELCOM, 2011a).[1] The damming of Finnish rivers started in southern Finland at the turn of the twentieth century and proceeded to the rural northern provinces from the 1940s onward (Autti & Karjalainen, 2012). Currently, almost all the major Finnish rivers discharging into the Baltic Sea are dammed. Fishways allowing Atlantic salmon to reach significant breeding habitats have been constructed only in the River Kymijoki, which now supports a wild – although non-native – Atlantic salmon population of River Neva origin (HELCOM, 2011a; Mäki-Petäys, Louhi, Orell, & Karjalainen, 2014). With these developments, Finland followed the lead of most industrialized countries globally (Vörösmarty et al., 2004).

Given the grim history of Finnish salmonid stocks, it is no surprise that the past decades have witnessed major political and legal efforts in several forums to restore ecological flows to the Finnish rivers. To reflect this, in 2012 the Finnish government issued a National Fishway Strategy aiming at restoring the natural reproductive cycle of migratory fish populations and prioritizing restorative actions in watersheds with the highest potential (Government of Finland, 2012). The uneasy relationship between migratory fish and hydropower has also attracted attention in the European Union and in international arenas. At present, the EU Water Framework Directive (WFD, 2000/60/EC) requires that EU member states reach good ecological status or good ecological potential in all inland waters by 2015 (or if postponed, by 2021, or 2027 at the latest). The vitality of migratory fish populations is among the 'biological quality elements' that contribute to the assessment of ecological status. Also, the Helsinki Commission, established by the 1992 Helsinki Convention,[2] has on several occasions expressed its concern for the state of Finnish rivers, and recommended that some of the old hydropower operations be re-evaluated (HELCOM, 2007).

In this article, we study the main legal and policy drivers that led to the large-scale damming of Finnish rivers and discuss why damming continues to be a problem for reviving migratory fish stocks today. Second, we study the legal, scientific and policy drivers for re-evaluating the fisheries obligations of the existing hydropower permits. We argue that there is a need for re-evaluation not only on the basis of international and EU legal obligations, but also because the science underlying the foundations on which permits were originally issued has developed significantly. Recent developments in law, science and policy constitute grounds for adjusting some of the existing hydropower permits in Finland. Theoretically speaking, this setting opens up a classical problem discussed in the adaptive law and governance literature: how to address law and past management decisions that are based on outdated and false assumptions about the functioning and development of social-ecological systems (e.g., Arnold & Gunderson, 2013; Cosens et al., 2017; Ruhl, 1997).

Overall, the uneasy relationship between biodiversity and hydropower has been well documented across the globe (Vörösmarty et al., 2004).[3] In a global context, the defects of Finnish hydropower governance offer a cautionary example of failure to manage the resilience of freshwater systems and adapt to global environmental change and the development of science. The current challenges in restoring and maintaining migratory salmonid stocks, and balancing them with the production of hydropower, trace back to three peculiarities of Finnish water law and policy. First, most of the present hydropower operations have their background in ad hoc legislation that permitted the large-scale damming of Finnish rivers in the 1930s and 1940s, a time of pressing societal and energy needs. Second, the laws under which the existing hydropower permits were issued (mostly between the 1930s and 1970s) were ambivalent as to the methods with which the impacts of hydropower on aquatic ecosystems and fisheries could be compensated (Hepola, 2007). Third, hydropower permits were granted permanence once issued (Belinskij & Soininen, 2017). These three characteristics have prevented new knowledge on the societal need for and the negative environmental consequences of hydropower from penetrating into water management practices.

Although this article concentrates on reconciling hydropower and fisheries biodiversity, research has shown that the reservoirs needed to store water for the production of hydropower have environmental impacts on a wider scale. Reservoirs not only destroy the natural landscape and reduce the flow of freshwater and organic material to the ocean, but also cause significant habitat fragmentation and act as an important source of greenhouse gas emissions due to the breakdown of organic material that accumulates in the reservoirs (Barros et al., 2011; Gagnon & van de Vate, 1997; Rosa, dos Santos, Matvienko, dos Santos, & Sikar, 2004; Rosenberg, Bodaly, & Usher, 1995; Vörösmarty et al., 2004). Reservoir construction also tends to lead to the leaching of mercury from immersed terrestrial soils and subsequent bacterial methylation in the reservoirs (Rosenberg et al., 1995). In addition to direct biogeochemical impacts, dams have reduced nutrient inputs from the sea to the rivers by blocking the spawning migration of fish (Jonsson & Jonsson, 2003). Absence of migratory fish has further caused local extinctions of species, such as freshwater pearl mussel (*Margaritifera margaritifera*), that are directly dependent on the presence of salmonid hosts (Karlsson, Larsen, & Hindar, 2014). The matter of regulating hydropower is further complicated by hydropower being a significant source of low-carbon energy. Against this background, the conflict between free-flowing rivers is not only between environment and development, but also between local environment (biodiversity) and global environment (climate mitigation).

Overall, the harms and the benefits of hydropower raise wide-ranging questions of law and policy, from both anthropocentric and ecocentric perspectives.[4] The present article concentrates, however, on studying Finland as a case of maladaptive water governance. Hopefully, this cautionary example can illuminate some characteristics that should be avoided in designing adaptive and effective water governance.

A history of losing the natural reproductive cycles of migratory fish in Finland

Ad hoc laws and insufficient fisheries compensation

Natural rivers provide many ecosystem services, including provisional services such as fish and flow to run turbines, regulation services such as flood mitigation and water purification, and cultural services such as recreation and aesthetic landscapes (Dyson, Bergkamp, & Scanlon, 2003). Typically, rivers host a variety of actors utilizing these services. As many of these uses are competing or conflicting, there is a need to manage the flows allocated for each use (Davis & Hirji, 2015; Dyson et al., 2003). 'Environmental flow' is a concept designed to strike a balance between the allocation of flows for different ecological and human uses (Gillespie, 2014). Within the EU context, the commission uses a narrower concept of 'ecological flow', which refers to the flows required to meet the WFD's ecological objectives (European Commission, 2015). This requires, among other things, that aquatic organisms can navigate rivers upstream and downstream.

The management of environmental flows in Finland has been largely dominated by the allocation of water for hydropower production. For most of the twentieth century, Finnish water policy and law leaned heavily towards allocating all the available water to the production of electricity (Belinskij & Soininen, 2017; Haataja, 1959). This was mostly due to hydropower being sorely needed to drive a growing – and after the Second World War crippled – economy (Pokka, 1991). A prevailing view within the industry in the 1930s and 1940s was that the allocation of water for any other purpose than the production of hydropower was frivolous and vain (Myllyntaus, 2002). This view came to dominate Finnish water policy and law for a long time.

Before the 1930s, the Water Rights Act (31/1902) had favoured fisheries over power. But as the demand for electricity increased over the years, interpretations of the 1902 act, and political pressure to pass legislation deviating from its strict rules, increased accordingly (Myllyntaus, 2002). The 1930s saw the dawning of a great recession, and by the end of the decade Finland entered World War II as a response to violent Soviet invasion (Pokka, 1991). These circumstances led to the introduction of ad hoc legislation that established far-reaching exemptions to the 1902 Water Rights Act (Pokka, 1991). In 1934–41, the Finnish Parliament passed four acts (62/1934; 134/1939; 383/1940; 196/1941) that permitted certain damming and regulation projects and lowered the criteria and procedural safeguards for permits to hydropower operations. The earlier ban on blocking a river's navigable fairway was replaced by a weighing norm requiring merely that the benefits of a project must outweigh the harms (Löyttyjärvi, 2013). If the economic value of a hydropower operation was great, the fisheries interests were sacrificed, with compensation (Legislative proposal 99/1938; Löyttyjärvi, 2013). All together, these legislative changes resulted in roughly half of Finnish hydropower capacity (61 operations with a combined output of 5400 GWh) being constructed before the enactment of the 1961 Water Act (Hinkka, 1969).

Despite the urgent need for electricity to fuel economic growth and the consequent prioritization of hydropower over environmental and societal impacts (Erkinaro et al., 2011), the laws at the time did contain provisions limiting construction on Finnish rivers. First of all, the operations were still subject to permitting, and the law required that hydropower-related harms to fisheries must be mitigated, minimized and compensated. Although the strict obligation of the 1902 Water Rights Act to compensate for hydropower harm to fisheries by building fishways was removed by the 1939 ad hoc legislation, fishways remained the main fisheries compensation mechanism in the Water Act (264/1961) well into the 1980s (Chapter 2, Section 22; Hepola, 2007).

Nevertheless, from the 1950s compensation practices started moving towards stocking rivers with farmed fish. This process was initiated because fishways and fish transfers were considered dysfunctional and expensive (Government of Finland, 2012; Hepola, 2007; Löyttyjärvi, 2013). A good illustration of this is that in the River Kemijoki – probably the most productive salmon river in Europe, until its damming soon after World War II – attempts were initially made to transfer ascending salmon over the dams, but the transfers turned out unsuccessful, and were later replaced by stocking of hatchery-reared fish (Alaniska, 2013). Compensatory stocking was legalized in 1987, when the 1961 Water Act was amended (amendment 467/1987). The amended act – read in light of the preparatory materials – prioritized stocking of farmed fish as the main method for compensating harm to fisheries (Legislative proposal 266/1984). At present, stocking still remains the main fisheries compensation method, despite the current Water Act (587/2011) giving the three compensation mechanisms of fishways, fish transfers and stocking equal weight (Chapter 3, Section 14; Legislative proposal 277/2009).

Taken together, the societal need to develop hydropower for energy security in the first half of the twentieth century was reflected closely in the four pieces of ad hoc legislation that were passed as exemptions to the 1902 Water Rights Act, which originally prohibited the blocking of river fairways. The laws that facilitated the large-scale development of hydropower required compensation for harm to fisheries, and these compensations evolved from the building of fishways towards stocking rivers or river mouths with farmed fish. While the societal significance of hydropower development in the shadow of recession and war was evident, the significance of shifting the compensatory mechanisms towards the stocking of farmed fish can only be understood in the historical light of biological understanding of fish and their genetic characteristics (see the section on 'Changes in Science').

Doctrine of permanence in hydropower permits

In addition to the large-scale river construction on the basis of dubious ad hoc legislation, the issued hydropower permits were granted permanence by Finnish water legislation. The 2011 Water Act and its predecessors (1961 Water Act; 1902 Water Rights Act 31/1902) are based on a strict *ex ante* ideology: once a hydropower operation is considered in a public process and granted a permit to operate, the permit cannot be revoked or greatly adjusted without the consent of the hydropower operator (Belinskij & Soininen, 2017). The permits granted to hydropower operations are considered to reflect the private ownership of the rivers, and the public evaluation of harm conducted in an original permit cannot be revisited after its assessment (Belinskij & Soininen, 2017; Hepola, 2005, 2007). This is not so much a procedural rule but a substantive one: permits cannot be considerably changed after the initial *ex ante* assessment.

On the basis of the permanence doctrine, the 2011 Water Act does not allow for entirely new permit conditions to be added to hydropower permits, if they were not present at the origin (Belinskij & Soininen, 2017). In particular, the permits for small (under 5 MW) hydropower operations quite often (38 operations out of 153 in total) lack conditions for compensating harm to fisheries (Kosunen & Mikkola, 2017). Furthermore, even the alteration of existing hydropower permit obligations is contingent on several rather strict legal criteria (Belinskij & Soininen, 2017). These criteria include the existence of a public interest in reviving migratory fish stocks (2011 Water Act, Chapter 19, Section 10), a change in the social-ecological circumstances (Chapter 3, Section 22), and a finding that the changes in permit obligations do not constitute disproportionate costs to the hydropower operator (Chapter 3, Section 21; Chapter 2, Section 7).

Overall, the 2011 Water Act and its predecessors have always had a dualistic approach to the development of policy and science. The law has been, and still is, remarkably adaptive to social-ecological knowledge in permitting *new* hydropower operations and deciding on their compensatory measures (Belinskij & Soininen, 2017; Haataja, 1951; Soininen, 2016). This close linkage between science, policy and law is, however, in stark contrast with the strict permanence of *existing* hydropower permits (Belinskij & Soininen, 2017; Hepola, 2005, 2007). The doctrine of permanence creates an atmosphere of maladaptivity that presents obstacles to adjusting past water management decisions to new developments in policy and law, as well as to new scientific knowledge.

The previous sections have sought to describe and evaluate some of the key historical reasons for the large-scale damming of Finnish rivers and explain how these historical developments continue to hold importance today. We next review the legal, scientific and policy arguments for a change in hydropower operations.

Flows of change: towards adjusting maladaptive regulation and permits?

Changes in law and context

In the first half of the twentieth century, hydropower was such a valuable commodity that it dominated over fisheries and other interests in the development and interpretation of water law in Finland. Hydropower accounted for roughly 90% of Finland's electricity production in the 1950s and 1960s (Finnish Energy, 2017), but since then, its contribution has decreased to the present 10–20% (Aslani, Naaranoja, Helo, Antila, & Hiltunen, 2013; Finnish Energy, 2017). But at the same time, the importance of hydropower's combined storage capacity has increased due to climate mitigation efforts and the development of fluctuating power sources, such as renewable wind, solar, and wave power (KEMA Consulting, 2015). Despite the diversification of hydropower's roles for climate change mitigation, energy security and some predicted growth in its electricity generation due to climate-change-induced increase in precipitation (Venäläinen et al., 2004), it is reasonable to assert that the societal importance and political sway of hydropower in Finland are substantially weaker now compared to its heyday in the 1950s and 1960s.

In the wake of hydropower's declining role in the Finnish energy mix, the last three decades have witnessed several political and legal attempts to balance hydropower and fisheries interests. The key political attempt in this regard is the National Fishway Strategy issued by the government of Finland in 2012. The strategy seeks to reconcile hydropower and fisheries interests, and recognizes that in the long term, healthy migratory fish populations can only be maintained by reviving their natural reproductive cycles (Government of Finland, 2012). To reach this overarching goal, the strategy proposes several measures, such as building fishways, watering dried-up channels, restoring dredged rivers, transferring fish over the existing dams, improving river flow regulation, and improving the regulation of fishing. It also recognizes that the permanence of hydropower permits (outlined in the previous section) stands in the way of these goals and measures.

Indeed, many legal attempts to balance hydropower and fisheries interests have not had significant success. While the two amendments of the 1961 Water Act (467/1987; 553/1994) introduced the possibility of adjusting ineffective fisheries compensation obligations in hydropower permits, the core of the permanence doctrine remained intact: no new conditions could be added to the existing permits. The current 2011 Water Act maintains the doctrine.

But, while the balancing of environmental flow allocation between hydropower and fisheries has been at an impasse for decades in Finland, this might be about to change due to EU law. The WFD requires all EU member states to reach good ecological status in all inland waters by 2015, or, if postponed, by 2021, or 2027 at the latest (Article 4(1); Squintani & van Rijswick, 2016). In the WFD system, the classification of ecological status in rivers is based on composition, abundance and age structure of fish fauna, among other biological quality elements (Annex V). Good ecological status of a river (or part of a river) requires, with regard to fish fauna, that there are only slight changes in species composition and abundance attributable to anthropogenic impacts. Hydro-morphological quality elements, such as the quantity and dynamics of water flow and river continuity, must also be considered.

These biological and hydro-morphological quality elements are somewhat different if a stretch of river is 'artificial and heavily modified' due to damming and the production of hydropower (Articles 2(9), 4(1)). In such case, the member state has an obligation to seek good ecological potential, which is established by comparing it to the maximum ecological potential of the water body. In practice, the latter refers to an ecological quality achievable 'once all mitigation measures, that do not have significant adverse effects on its specified use [here: hydropower] or on the wider environment, have been applied' (WFD CIS Guidance Document No. 4, 2003). Good ecological potential requires that there are only slight changes in quality elements as compared to the maximum ecological potential.

The WFD requires that member states re-evaluate all the existing impoundment and other water management permits to bridge the gap between the existing status and good ecological status/potential of all waters in their territory (Articles 11(3), 11(5)). In the *Weser* ruling, the Court of Justice of the EU declared that the environmental goals of the WFD are legally binding in relation to the authorization of an individual project (Case 461/13, *Bund für Umwelt und Naturschutz Deutschland eV v Bundesrepublik Deutschland* [2015] ECLI:EU:C:2015). While the legally binding nature of good ecological status may introduce far-reaching legal consequences for the re-evaluation of existing permits, good ecological potential sets more modest standards for heavily modified rivers. Attaining good ecological potential does not require cancelling hydropower permits or removing dams, but it might well require a wide array of ecological compensation mechanisms to allow the natural reproductive cycle for salmon and trout as far as technically possible, and economically feasible. These measures may include building fishways, watering original drained channels, restoring dredged rivers, transferring fish over the dams, and improving river flow regulation, as listed in the National Fishway Strategy (Government of Finland, 2012).

Most of the Finnish rivers dammed for hydropower have been classified as artificial and heavily modified. But, notwithstanding their less demanding ecological quality criteria, 66% of the artificial and heavily modified rivers (or parts of rivers) in Finland were not in compliance with good ecological potential in the first WFD planning period, between 2004 and 2009 (Finnish Environment Institute, 2013). Against this background, the directive's obligations cast a long shadow, especially on those hydropower permits that do not presently contain any fisheries compensation obligations. Stocking of farmed fish may not be enough to produce good ecological potential.

The dire situation of salmon and trout in Finland has also attracted some attention in the context of international law, mainly under the 1992 Helsinki Convention. In the 2007 Baltic Sea Action Plan, the Baltic Sea states agreed to develop restoration plans for migratory routes and spawning sites to reach favourable conservation status in Baltic Sea biodiversity (HELCOM, 2007). HELCOM has also recommended that the states take urgent measures for the recovery of the original salmon and sea trout populations (HELCOM, 2011b). In this regard, Finland should assess anthropogenic hindrances to fish migration in its territory and commit to re-establishing wild salmon populations in certain rivers where justified (HELCOM, 2011b).

Overall, the legal and policy developments at all levels (national, EU, international) have sought to establish a balance between the social and ecological uses of environmental flows. The WFD especially is applying significant pressure toward changing Finnish water and fisheries management regulation and practices. This pressure is felt especially in the requirement to use a full array of fisheries compensation mechanisms (fishways, fish transfers, restocking) in aspiration toward good ecological status/potential. In light of this, the above analysis contests the doctrine of permanence of hydropower permits, especially if the permit does not contain any fisheries compensation obligations.

In the next section, we show how – in addition to law and policy – science has changed considerably since the time most of the Finnish hydropower permits were issued (between the 1930s and 1970s). Our argument here is that all the existing permits are, to a certain extent, based on an overoptimistic (and thus dismissive) evaluation of hydropower's harm to the environment in general, and fisheries in particular.

Changes in science: (re-)evaluating hydropower impacts and fisheries compensation

While it is evident that the environmental impacts of hydropower and the smolt production capacity of the impacted rivers (Romakkaniemi, 2008) were originally underestimated, research has also cast serious doubt on whether hydropower's harm to fisheries can be sustainably compensated by releasing farmed fish. At the time of early dam building (before the 1970s), there was little understanding of the importance of genetic diversity, microevolution or local adaptations in fish. Evolution was considered something that takes millions of years, though the current view is that ecologically significant genetic changes can occur in 10 or fewer generations (Hard et al., 2008; Rice & Emery, 2003; Schoener, 2011). Understanding of the importance of genetic factors was further hindered by the strict view that an evolutionary change cannot be inferred from a phenotypic change without direct genetic evidence (Merilä & Hendry, 2014).

The management implications of population genetic differences among brown trout populations were generally realized in the early 1980s (Taggart, Ferguson, & Mason, 1981). Ferguson and Mason (1981) were among the first to demonstrate that brown trout morphotypes formed reproductively isolated sub-populations, even in the same waterbody. From the late 1980s, awareness of the population-genetic structures of fish in general and salmonids in particular started to grow (Hallerman & Beckmann, 1988). Taylor (1991) concluded that the ample genetic variation among stocks and strays was potentially largely adaptive, with apparent concern for the increasing rates of fish releases and escapees from fish farms. Bourke, Coughlan, Jansson, Galvin, and Cross (1997) pointed out that hatchery releases of Atlantic salmon could compromise the original Europe-wide genetic variation in Atlantic salmon populations. In addition, there was increasing concern that hatchery-rearing could favour traits such as fast growth or early maturation, affecting the productivity of the sea-ranched stocks (Kallio-Nyberg & Koljonen, 1997). However, it has taken until very recently for the full-scale genomic diversity among populations (Lemopoulos et al., 2018) and the genetic basis for traits such as migration timing to be revealed in salmonids (Cauwelier, Gilbey, Sampayo, Stradmeyer, & Middlemas, 2018).

Despite the lack of modern genetic methods in the 1970s, biologists were concerned that hatchery-rearing might change the heritable traits of fish. For example, it was reported in 1977 that hatchery-reared steelhead trout (*Oncorhynchus mykiss*) had differences in growth and survival compared to wild trout and wild × hatchery hybrids (Reisenbichler & McIntyre, 1977). The first papers that reported that hatchery-rearing might have caused loss of genetic diversity due to genetic drift and the small number of founders used in establishing hatchery broodstocks appeared in the 1980s (Cross & King, 1983; Ryman & Ståhl, 1980; Vuorinen, 1984).

While the positive association between the genetic diversity and the vitality of various animal populations has been long known (Hutchings & Fraser, 2008), there were no studies on the fitness consequences of hatchery-rearing until the 2000s. Tiira, Piironen, and Primmer (2006) observed that a lack of genetic diversity was associated with malformations in landlocked Lake Saimaa salmon juveniles, and Araki, Cooper, and Blouin (2007) showed that the genetic effects of domestication reduced the subsequent reproductive capabilities of steelhead trout by ca. 40% per captive-reared generation when fish were moved to their natural environments. In the 2010s, the modern functional genomics approaches have developed quickly: Vasemägi, Kahar, and Ozerov (2016) demonstrated directly that different genes contributed to the fast growth of salmon in the wild, compared to a hatchery environment. Christie, Marine, Fox, French, and Blouin (2016) showed that just a single generation of hatchery breeding altered the expression of hundreds of genes in steelhead trout.

Currently, it is not a scientific question whether hatchery-rearing has negative genetic impacts on fish (Araki, Berejikian, Ford, & Blouin, 2008; Araki et al., 2007; Christie et al., 2016; Hansen, Meier, & Mensberg, 2010; Kallio-Nyberg, Jutila, Jokikokko, & Saloniemi, 2006). Rather, the question is how long hatchery breeding and the current restocking practices can support fisheries at feasible economic costs (Hutchings & Fraser, 2008).

While the scientific evidence for negative hatchery-induced genetic effects is solid, one is left wondering what the practical implications are. For example, the final power plant that destroyed all the remaining breeding grounds of landlocked Lake Saimaa salmon was constructed in 1971 (Pursiainen, Makkonen, & Piironen, 1998). This was roughly a decade before the genetic diversity of salmonid populations in general – and the significant losses of genetic diversity already during the first years of hatchery rearing in Lake Saimaa brown trout and landlocked Atlantic salmon – were revealed (Vuorinen, 1982, 1984). Thus, the apparent future-looking answer is that the current large-scale stocking severely threatens the small remaining wild populations.

Stocking induces homogenization of genetic structures and loss of local adaptations as well as phenotypic changes in a multitude of traits (Hansen et al., 2010; Palmé, Wennerström, Guban, & Laikre, 2012; Vainikka, Kallio-Nyberg, Heino, & Koljonen, 2010). Genetic changes in captive-bred fish can significantly lower restocking success and limit the possibility of restoring the salmon and trout populations in rivers that have lost their original fish. Virtually no examples of self-sustaining migratory salmonid populations with stocking origin exist in Finland, with the exception of the River Kymijoki salmon, which breed in low numbers.

The present knowledge of genetic harm caused by hatchery rearing is fully in line with the success of stocking over the past decades. Early stocking in both the Baltic Sea and inland waters produced good catches with generally high recapture rates (International Council for the Exploration of the Sea, 2011). As recently as in the 1990s, compensatory stocking supported intensive commercial salmon and anadromous brown trout fisheries in the Baltic Sea. More than 5 million salmon smolts were released annually, and the sea ranching produced peak salmon catches of ca. 5.5 million kg in the early 1990s. In the 1980s, the post-smolt survival of hatchery-reared salmon was 20–30% (HELCOM, 2011a). Commercial fisheries based on sea-ranching of hatchery-released salmon smolts started to decline from the 1990s onward. Much of the decline in catches was explained by the decreasing survival rates of stocked Baltic salmon (HELCOM, 2011a). Although several environmental changes – including climate change, the increase of seal and cormorant populations, and overfishing of Baltic cod, with effects on salmon diet – have also had ecological impacts on the survival of wild salmon and sea trout post-smolts, these alone cannot account for the extremely low survival rates of the stocked smolts (Kallio-Nyberg et al., 2006; Salminen, 2002).

While there is no direct genetic evidence that unintended domestication explains the decreased recapture rates of stocked fish, there is no solid evidence to reject the hypothesis either. Overall, the very low recapture rate and the inadvertent genetic impacts of stocked smolts have challenged the prevailing stocking practices (Erkinaro et al., 2011; Ozerov et al., 2016). Many Finnish salmon and trout broodstocks have now been maintained in hatcheries for 6 to 10 generations. In theory, this is the time after which the negative genetic effects would start to become significant (Hutchings & Fraser, 2008). Genetic evidence from the Estonian River Selja, which was recolonized by salmon from neighbouring rivers in 1990s and by stocking since 1997, after prior heavy pollution and extinction of the original salmon population, suggests that wild fish are more important in rebuilding a new population than stocked fish, even if the stocked fish outnumber the wild fish by an order of magnitude (Vasemägi et al., 2001).

In a broader context, populations of wild migratory salmonids are affected by numerous anthropogenic factors. For example, the major global threats to wild Atlantic salmon include (in addition to dam construction and stocking of hatchery-reared smolts) over-fishing, river engineering, pollution and salmon aquaculture. Forseth et al. (2017) identified escaped farmed salmon and salmon lice (*Lepeophtheirus salmonis*) from fish farms as *emerging* population threats in Norway, and *Gyrodactylus salaris* parasite, freshwater acidification, hydropower regulation and other habitat alterations as *stabilized* threats. The threats vary regionally, and in the Baltic Sea basin, the management of stocking and sea ranching has been classified as the most urgent concern (Palmé et al., 2012).

In conclusion, although it would be anachronistic and vain to criticize the historical hydropower and fisheries management decisions that led to the damming of Finnish rivers, the loss of natural fish populations and the triumph of hatchery-reared fish, a strong argument can be made that those decisions should be reconsidered in today's social-ecological context and under current scientific knowledge. If one is serious about restoring the natural reproductive cycles of salmon and trout, as one must be based on the present analysis, the harmful impacts of using hatchery-reared fish in compensating for hydropower harm must be considered.

Discussion and a way forward

After the hydropower boom in Finland, two interrelated challenges remain in reviving the reproductive cycles of migratory fish – one biological, and the other related to law and policy. From a biological perspective, the original migratory salmonid populations in dammed rivers have become extinct, and their original genetic characteristics may not be recoverable, even if some subset of the original genetic variation has been maintained in the fish hatcheries. This means that, instead of simple population recovery, the challenge is to re-introduce and establish new populations in rivers that are open to fish migration. Such a task is not trivial and will need evolutionary thinking and consideration of the adaptive potential of the fish strain used for re-introductory stocking (Rice & Emery, 2003). While the conservation status of a species can be regionally improved by creating new populations, nothing will bring back the unique population-genetic units, with their original river-specific characteristics, once they are lost.

The legal and policy challenges include questions as to whether and to what extent hatchery-impacted stocks can recover in rivers that are potentially subjected to the re-evaluation of the hydropower permits and compensation measures. Thus, the apparent question is whether compensation measures should be taken nationally, in rivers where the opportunities for the recovery of native populations are better. Damming's local harm to the landscape cannot be compensated for anywhere else, but aquatic ecosystem diversity at the national scale could be maximized by taking action where the cost–benefit ratio is the best. This would require a new national-level compensation mechanism and fisheries fees collected from all hydropower companies.

At present, most of the Finnish rivers do not support natural salmonid life-cycles, and movement towards the goals of the WFD and the Baltic Sea Action Plan has been slow. Overall, the pressure from the EU and international arenas has not yet been strong enough to produce significant changes in the Finnish legal system. Despite this, the last two decades have witnessed several modest attempts to reallocate environmental flows. The legal framework of the EU does require the utilization of a broader array of fisheries compensation mechanisms than those in use in Finland at the moment.

Under the WFD, there is an obligation to evaluate whether the compensation mechanisms set in the permit conditions are adequate in relation to the environmental objectives of the directive. To this end, some administrative processes grounded in the 2011 Water Act may change existing hydropower permits by introducing new fishways and fish transfers and restoring breeding habitats (Lapin ELY-keskus, 2017). With these grass-roots developments, it remains to be seen whether the Finnish legal framework is flexible enough to allow changes in implementing obligations stemming from the EU, international law and conservation science. The slow progress towards balancing hydropower interests and aquatic biodiversity is a testament to the uneasy relationship between permanent water permits on the one hand, and adaptive management of rivers on the other. Laws once passed and management decisions once made cast a long shadow into the future. For this reason, balancing permanence and adaptivity becomes a key question in designing effective and legitimate water governance. The Finnish example leaves a lot to be desired in this regard.

Notes

1. In addition, intensive forestry operations – including the transformation of 6 million hectares of wetlands into ditched forests, and the dredging of rivers for timber floating – have altered the chemical and structural composition of the rivers over the last century or so and eliminated a significant number of breeding habitats for salmon and trout (HELCOM, 2011a). Restoration of river habitats has helped mitigate harm caused by the dredging of rivers, but the conflict between hydropower operations and restoring the natural reproductive cycle of migratory fish remains at a standstill (HELCOM, 2011a).
2. Convention on the Protection of the Marine Environment of the Baltic Sea Area, entered into force 17 January 2000.
3. The Columbia River in the western United States in one of the best-known examples (Dietrich, 2003; National Research Council, 1996; Williams, 2006).
4. New Zealand and Ecuador are among the first countries to grant rivers legal personhood (Scientific American, 2017).

Disclosure statement

No potential conflict of interest was reported by the authors.

Funding

This work was supported by the Strategic Research Council of Finland under projects Winland and BlueAdapt.

References

Alaniska, K. (2013). The extinction of the king of fishes. Kemijoki powerplants construction and the issue of the migratory fishes 1943–1964. Retrieved December 20, 2017, from http://jultika. oulu.fi/files/isbn9789526202518.pdf

Araki, H., Berejikian, B. A., Ford, M. J., & Blouin, M. S. (2008). Fitness of hatchery-reared salmonids in the wild. *Evolutionary Applications, 1*, 342–355.

Araki, H., Cooper, B., & Blouin, M. S. (2007). Genetic effects of captive breeding cause a rapid, cumulative fitness decline in the wild. *Science, 318*, 100–103.

Arnold, G. A., & Gunderson, L. H. (2013). Adaptive Law and Resilience. *Environmental Law Reporter, 43*, 10426–10443.

Aslani, A., Naaranoja, M., Helo, P., Antila, E., & Hiltunen, E. (2013). Energy diversification in Finland: Achievements and potential of renewable energy development. *International Journal of Sustainable Energy, 32*, 504–514.

Autti, O., & Karjalainen, T. P. (2012). The point of no return – Social dimensions of losing salmon in two northern rivers. *Nordia Geographical Publications, 41*, 45–56.

Barros, N., Cole, J. J., Tranvik, L. J., Prairie, Y. T., Bastviken, D., Huszar, L. M., … Roland, F. (2011). Carbon emission from hydroelectric reservoirs linked to reservoir age and latitude. *Nature Geoscience, 4*, 593–596.

Belinskij, A., & Soininen, N. (2017). Bringing back ecological flows. The case of migratory fish and the regulation of hydropower in Finland. *Ympäristöpolitiikan ja -oikeuden vuosikirja, 10*, 89–149. (in Finnish).

Bourke, E. A., Coughlan, J., Jansson, H., Galvin, P., & Cross, T. F. (1997). Allozyme variation in population of Atlantic salmon located throughout Europe: Diversity that could be compromised by introductions of reared fish. *ICES Journal of Marine Science, 54*, 974–985.

Cauwelier, E., Gilbey, J., Sampayo, J., Stradmeyer, L., & Middlemas, S. J. (2018). Identification of a single genomic region associated with seasonal river return timing in adult Scottish Atlantic salmon (*Salmo salar*), using a genome-wide association study. *Canadian Journal of Fisheries and Aquatic Sciences, 75*, 1427–1435.

Christie, M. R., Marine, M. L., Fox, S. E., French, R. A., & Blouin, M. S. (2016). A single generation of domestication heritably alters the expression of hundreds of genes. *Nature Communications, 7*, 10676.

Cosens, B. A., Craig, R. K., Hirsch, S., Arnold, C. A. T., Benson, M. H., DeCaro, D. A., ... Schlager, E. (2017). The role of law in adaptive governance. *Ecology and Society, 22*(1), 1–30.

Cross, T. F., & King, J. (1983). Genetic effects of hatchery rearing in Atlantic salmon. *Aquaculture, 33*, 33–40.

Davis, R., & Hirji, R. (eds.). (2015). *Environmental flows: Concepts and methods.* Washington, DC: The World Bank.

Dietrich, W. (2003). *Northwest passage: The mighty Columbia.* Seattle, WA: University of Washington Press.

Dyson, M., Bergkamp, G., & Scanlon, J. (eds.). (2003). *Flow. The essentials of environmental flows.* Gland, Switzerland and Cambridge, UK: IUCN.

Erkinaro, J., Laine, A., Mäki-Petäys, A., Karjalainen, T. P., Laajala, E., Hirvonen, A., ... Yrjänä, T. (2011). Restoring migratory salmonid populations in regulated rivers in the northernmost Baltic Sea area, Northern Finland - biological, technical and social challenges. *Journal of Applied Ichthyology, 27*(Suppl. 3), 45–52.

European Commission. (2015). *Ecological flows in the implementation of the Water Framework Directive* (Guidance Document No. 31).

Ferguson, A., & Mason, F. M. (1981). Allozyme evidence for reproductively isolated sympatric populations of brown trout *Salmo trutta* L. in Lough Melvin, Ireland. *Journal of Fish Biology, 18*, 629–642.

Finnish Energy. (2017). Vesivoimalla eniten uusiutuvaa sähköntuotantoa. Retrieved November 29, 2017, from https://energia.fi/perustietoa_energia-alasta/energiantuotanto/sahkontuotanto/vesivoima

Finnish Environment Institute. (2013). Vesienhoidon suunnittelun ohjeistus 2. kaudelle. Voimakkaasti muutettujen ja keinotekoisten pintavesien tunnistaminen ja tilan arviointi. Retrieved November 29, 2017, from http://www.ymparisto.fi/download/noname/%7B755CCAF4-99E3-46F9-AB0C-E38B90A2E924%7D/74887

Forseth, T., Barlaup, B. T., Finstad, B., Fiske, P., Gjøsæter, H., Falkegård, M., ... Wennevik, V. (2017). The major threats to Atlantic salmon in Norway. *ICES Journal of Marine Science, 74*, 1496–1513.

Gagnon, L., & van de Vate, J. F. (1997). Greenhouse gas emissions from hydropower: The state of research in 1996. *Energy Policy, 25*, 7–13.

Gillespie, B. (2014). What are environmental flows? The River Management Blog. Retrieved November 27, 2017, from https://therivermanagementblog.wordpress.com/2014/04/28/what-are-environmental-flows/

Government of Finland. (2012). Kansallinen kalatiestrategia. Valtioneuvoston periaatepäätös 8.3.2012. Retrieved November 21, 2017, from http://mmm.fi/documents/1410837/1516655/1-4-Kansallinen_kalatiestrategia2012.pdf/fae1c9f2-2908-4859-82ce-0b46c612f179

Haataja, K. (1951). *Vesioikeus I.* Porvoo: Suomalainen Lakimiesyhdistys.

Haataja, K. (1959). *Vesioikeus III.* Helsinki: Suomalainen Lakimiesyhdistys.

Hallerman, E. M., & Beckmann, J. S. (1988). DNA-Level polymorphism as a tool in fisheries science. *Canadian Journal of Fisheries and Aquatic Sciences, 45*, 1075–1087.

Hansen, M. M., Meier, K., & Mensberg, K.-L. D. (2010). Identifying footprints of selection in stocked brown trout populations: A spatio-temporal approach. *Molecular Ecology, 19*, 1787–1800.

Hard, J. J., Gross, M. R., Heino, M., Hilborn, R., Kope, R. G., Law, R., & Reynolds, J. D. (2008). Evolutionary consequences of fishing and their implications for salmon. *Evolutionary Applications, 1*, 388–408.

HELCOM. (2007). *Baltic Sea Action Plan*. Adopted on 15 November 2007 in Krakow, Poland by the HELCOM Extraordinary Ministerial Meeting.

HELCOM. (2011a). Salmon and Sea Trout Populations and Rivers in the Baltic Sea – HELCOM assessment of salmon (*Salmo salar*) and sea trout (*Salmo trutta*) populations and habitats in rivers flowing to the Baltic Sea. *Baltic Sea Environment Protection* No. 126A.

HELCOM. (2011b). HELCOM recommendation 32-33/1. Adopted 15 June 2011.

Hepola, M. (2005). *Oikeusvoimaopin transformaatio. Siviiliprosessioikeudellisen oikeusvoimaopin muuttuminen ja siirtyminen hallinto- ja ympäristöoikeuteen ympäristöluvan pysyvyyden kannalta*. Helsinki: Edilex.

Hepola, M. (2007). Kalatalousvelvoite muutoksen tuulissa. In J. Eklund (Ed.), *Vesi, ympäristö ja oikeus: Juhlakirja Pekka Kainlaurille* (pp. 209–265). Vaasa: Vaasan Hallinto-oikeus.

Hinkka, R. O. (1969). Oikeudet rakennettavaan vesivoimaan. In R. Salokangas (Ed.), *Suomen vesivoima*. Helsinki: Suomen Vesivoimayhdistys.

Hutchings, J. A., & Fraser, D. J. (2008). The nature of fisheries- and farming-induced evolution. *Molecular Ecology, 17*, 294–313.

International Council for the Exploration of the Sea. (2011). Report of the Working Group on Baltic Salmon and Trout (WGBAST). ICES Advisory Committee. ICES 2011/ACOM:08.

Jonsson, B., & Jonsson, N. (2003). Migratory Atlantic salmon as vectors for the transfer of energy and nutrients between freshwater and marine environments. *Freshwater Biology, 48*, 21–27.

Kallio-Nyberg, I., Jutila, E., Jokikokko, E., & Saloniemi, I. (2006). Survival of reared Atlantic salmon and sea trout in relation to marine conditions of smolt year in the Baltic Sea. *Fisheries Research, 80*, 295–304.

Kallio-Nyberg, I., & Koljonen, M.-L. (1997). The genetic consequence of hatchery-rearing on life-history traits of the Atlantic salmon (Salmo salar L.): A comparative analysis of sea-ranched salmon with wild and reared parents. *Aquaculture, 153*, 207–224.

Karlsson, S., Larsen, B. M., & Hindar, K. (2014). Host-dependent genetic variation in freshwater pearl mussel (*Margaritifera margaritifera* L.). *Hydrobiologia, 735*, 179–190.

KEMA Consulting. (2015). The hydropower sector's contribution to a sustainable and prosperous Europe. Main Report On behalf of: A European Hydropower Initiative of Hydropower Companies and (supported by) Associations. Retrieved November 29, 2017, from https://energia.fi/files/507/Main_Report_-_Macro-Economic_Study_on_Hydropower_in_Europe.pdf

Kosunen, N., & Mikkola, I. (2017). *Selvitys Suomen alle 5 MW vesivoimalaitosten sekä niihin välittömästi liittyvien säännöstelyhankkeiden vesilain mukaisten lupien kalatalousvelvoitteista*. Linnunmaa Oy.

Lapin ELY-keskus. (2017). Hakemus 17.3.2017:Kemijoen Isohaaran, Taivalkosken, Ossauskosken, Petäjäskosken, Valajaskosken, Vanttauskosken, Pirttikosken ja Seitakorvan sekä Raudanjoen Permantokosken voimalaitosten kalatalousvelvoitteiden muuttaminen.

Legislative proposals:
- Legislative proposal HE 266/1984 vp. Hallituksen esitys eduskunnalle laiksi vesilain muuttamisesta.
- Legislative proposal HE 277/2009 vp. Hallituksen esitys eduskunnalle vesilainsäädännön uudistamiseksi.
- Legislative proposal HE 99/1938 vp. Hallituksen esitys laiksi vesioikeuslain muuttamisesta.

Lemopoulos, A., Uusi-Heikkilä, S., Vasemägi, A., Huusko, A., Kokko, H., & Vainikka, A., (2018). Genome-wide divergence patterns support fine-scaled genetic structuring associated with migration tendency in brown trout. *Canadian Journal of Fisheries and Aquatic Sciences, 75*, 1680–1692.

Löyttyjärvi, M.-L. (2013). Vesivoima omaisuutena ja virtavesi elinympäristönä. *Ympäristöjuridiikka, 1*, 30–60.

Mäki-Petäys, A., Louhi, P., Orell, P., & Karjalainen, T. P. (2014). *Rakennettujen jokien tutkimusohjelma: Väliraportti 2010–2013* (RKTL:ntyöraportteja 13/2014). Helsinki: Riista- ja kalatalouden tutkimuslaitos.

Merilä, J., & Hendry, A. P. (2014). Climate change, adaptation, and phenotypic plasticity: The problem and the evidence. *Evolutionary Applications, 7*, 1–14.

Myllyntaus, T. (2002). Kalastus ja vesien virkistyskäyttö. *Vesitalous, 5*, 29–32.

National Research Council. (1996). *Upstream: Salmon and society in the Pacific Northwest.* Washington, D.C.: National Academy Press.

Ozerov, M. Y., Gross, R., Bruneaux, M., Vähä, J.-P., Burimski, O., Pukk, L., & Vasemägi, A. (2016). Genomewide introgressive hybridization patterns in wild Atlantic salmon incluenced by inadvertent gene flow from hatchery releases. *Molecular Ecology, 25*, 1275–1293.

Palmé, A., Wennerström, L., Guban, P., & Laikre, L. (eds.) (2012). Stopping compensatory releases of salmon in the Baltic Sea. Good or bad for Baltic salmon gene pools? *Report from the Baltic Salmon 2012 symposium and workshop*, Sweden: Stockholm University.

Pokka, H. (1991). *Rakennettujen vesistöjen jälkivalvontajärjestelmät.* Helsinki: Suomalainen Lakimiesyhdistys.

Pursiainen, M., Makkonen, J., & Piironen, J. (1998). Maintenance and exploitation of landlocked salmon, *Salmo salar* m. *sebago*, in the Vuoksi watercourse. In I. G. Cowx (Ed.), *Stocking and introduction of fish*. Oxford: Fishing News Books.

Rassi, P., HyväRinen, E., Juslén, A., & Mannerkoski, I. (eds.). (2010). *The 2010 red list of finnish species.* Helsinki: Ympäristöministeriö & Suomen ympäristökeskus.

Reisenbichler, R. R., & McIntyre, J. D. (1977). Genetic differences in growth and survival of juvenile hatchery and wild steelhead trout, *Salmo gairdneri. Canadian Journal of Fisheries and Aquatic Sciences, 34*, 123–128.

Rice, K. J., & Emery, N. C. (2003). Managing microevolution: Restoration in the face of global change. *Frontiers in Ecology and the Environment, 1*, 469–478.

Romakkaniemi, A. (2008). *Conservation of Atlantic salmon by supplementary stocking of juvenile fish* (Phd Thesis). Helsinki: University of Helsinki and Finnish Game and Fisheries Research Institute.

Rosa, L. P., dos Santos, M. A., Matvienko, B., dos Santos, E. O., & Sikar, E. (2004). Greenhouse Gas Emissions from Hydroelectric Reservoirs in Tropical Regions. *Climatic Change, 66*, 9–21.

Rosenberg, D. M., Bodaly, R. A., & Usher, P. J. (1995). Environmental and social impacts of large scale hydroelectric development: Who is listening? *Global Environmental Change, 5*, 127–148.

Ruhl, J. B. (1997). Thinking of environmental law as a complex adaptive system: How to clean up the environment by making a mess of environmental law. *Houston Law Review, 34*, 933–1002.

Ryman, N., & Ståhl, G. (1980). Genetic changes in hatchery stocks of brown trout (*Salmo trutta*). *Canadian Journal of Fisheries and Aquatic Sciences, 37*, 82–87.

Salminen, M. (2002). Marine survival of Atlantic salmon in the Baltic Sea. NPACF Technical Report No. 4. Causes of Marine Mortality of Salmon in the North Pacific and North Atlantic Oceans and in the Baltic Sea. 2002 Joint Meeting on Causes of Marine Mortality of Salmon in the North Pacific and North Atlantic Oceans and in the Baltic Sea. March 14–15, 2002, Vancouver, British Columbia, Canada.

Schoener, T. W. (2011). The newest synthesis: Understanding the interplay of evolutionary and ecological dynamics. *Science, 331*, 426–429.

Scientific American. (2017). Rivers Get Human Rights: They Can Sue to Protect Themselves. Retrieved April 16, 2018, from https://www.scientificamerican.com/article/rivers-get-human-rights-they-can-sue-to-protect-themselves/

Soininen, N. (2016). *Transparencies in legality: A legal analysis of the reason-giving requirement in water management permitting in Finland.* Helsinki: Suomalainen Lakimiesyhdistys.

Squintani, L., & van Rijswick, H. (2016). Improving legal certainty and adaptability in the programmatic approach. *Journal of Environmental Law, 28*, 443–470.

Taggart, J., Ferguson, A., & Mason, F. M. (1981). Genetic variation in Irish populations of brown trout (*Salmo trutta* L.): Electrophoretic analysis of allozymes. *Comparative Biochemistry and Physiology B, 69*, 393–412.

Taylor, E. B. (1991). A review of local adaptation in Salmonidae, with particular reference to Pacific and Atlantic salmon. *Aquaculture, 98*, 185–207.

Tiira, K., Piironen, J., & Primmer, C. R. (2006). Evidence for reduced genetic variation in severely deformed juvenile salmonids. *Canadian Journal of Fisheries and Aquatic Sciences, 63*, 2700–2707.

Vainikka, A., Kallio-Nyberg, I., Heino, M., & Koljonen, M.-L. (2010). Divergent trends in life-history traits between Atlantic salmon, *Salmo salar* of wild and hatchery origin in the Baltic Sea. *Journal of Fish Biology, 76*, 622–640.

Vasemägi, A., Gross, R., Paaver, T., Kangur, M., Nilsson, J., & Eriksson, L. O. (2001). Identification of the origin of an Atlantic salmon (Salmo salar L.) population in a recently recolonized river in the Baltic Sea. *Molecular Ecology, 10*, 2877–2882.

Vasemägi, A., Kahar, S., & Ozerov, M. Y. (2016). Genes that affect Atlantic salmon growth in hatchery do not have the same effect in the wild. *Functional Ecology, 30*, 1687–1695.

Venäläinen, A., Tammelin, B., Tuomenvirta, H., Jylhä, K., Koskela, J., Turunen, M. A., … Järvinen, P. (2004). The influence of climate change on energy production & heating energy demand in Finland. *Energy & Environment, 15*, 93–109.

Vörösmarty, C., Lettenmaier, D., Leveque, C., Meybeck, M., Pahl-Wostl, C., Alcamo, J., … Naiman, R. (2004). Humans transforming the global water system. *Eos, Transactions American Geophysical Union, 85*, 509–514.

Vuorinen, J. (1982). Little genetic variation in the Finnish Lake salmon, *Salmo salar Sebago* (Girard). *Hereditas, 97*, 189–192.

Vuorinen, J. (1984). Reduction of genetic variability in a hatchery stock of brown trout, *Salmo trutta* L. *Journal of Fish Biology, 24*, 339–348.

WFD CIS Guidance Document No. 4. (2003). Identification and Designation of Heavily Modified and Artificial Water Bodies.

Williams, R. N. (2006). *Return to the River – Restoring Salmon to the Columbia River*. Burlington, MA, US: Elsevier Academic Press.

Forestry management and water law: comparing Ecuador and Arizona

Andrés Martínez Moscoso 🆔 and Rhett Larson 🆔

ABSTRACT

This article compares public–private partnerships dedicated to improving forestry management to protect water in the Paute River basin in Ecuador (FONAPA) and the Verde River basin in Arizona (the Four Forest Restoration Initiative). Both programmes create incentives for improved forestry management and suggest lessons for water management in general but may face legal challenges that require reforms. While there is scope for mutual learning between the programmes, such cross-fertilization is inhibited by differences in the legal status of water and forest resources in the two systems.

Introduction

At first glance, one might think that the nation of Ecuador and the US state of Arizona have little in common with respect to water resource management. Although the two jurisdictions are similar in size, Ecuador is famed for its geographic diversity – ranging from rainforest to coastal mangrove swamps and highland *páramos* (high plateaus in the Andes Mountains between the tree line and snow line). Ecuador sits atop the Andes mountain range and at the headwaters of the largest river on the planet, the Amazon. On the other hand, Arizona is largely an arid region famous for the Grand Canyon, carved out of desert mountain rock by the Colorado River. Nevertheless, they share one particular water challenge. Both jurisdictions have large upland forests that play a critical role in water resource management. The forests in Ecuador and Arizona, like many such ecosystems around the world, are also threatened by climate change and population growth (Goldman, Benitez, Calvache, & Ramos, 2010). Greater investments in forests, as 'green infrastructure' providing critical ecosystem services in water protection, are essential to respond to these challenges (Echevarria, Zavala, Coronel, Montalvo, & Aguirre, 2015). This article examines recent legal innovations in river basins in Ecuador and Arizona, which aim to promote improved forestry management, or 'green infrastructure', for the protection of water supplies. This article compares and contrasts these different approaches and suggests lessons from each programme that might improve management in both jurisdictions.

Water law and regulations in Ecuador and Arizona

This section describes the importance of forests in watershed management and gives an overview of relevant water law and regulations in Arizona and Ecuador to establish a foundation for understanding how reforms can improve forestry management and to compare the approaches taken by each jurisdiction.

The relationship between forests and water quality and supply

Forests and water are so interconnected that forestry management is sometimes referred to as watershed management (Larson, 2016). While broader definitions could be used, for the purposes of this article, 'watershed management refers to removal of vegetation from a catchment, such as scrub brush or invasive species, as a part of a broader timber harvest plan' (McConkey, 1994). Watershed management has several potential benefits. First, removal of scrub brush and immature trees can improve forest health by allowing other trees to reach full maturity (McConkey, 1994). Second, this removal may help avoid or mitigate wildfire risks and insect infestation like bark beetles (Larson, 2016). Third, better forest health and fewer wildfires can reduce erosion and runoff to rivers, improving water quality (Larson, 2016). Fourth, removing vegetation from the watershed at a responsible rate can increase streamflow, augmenting water supplies (McConkey, 1994). Healthy forests protect winter snowpack from melting too fast, and from losing precipitation to immediate evaporation (Hibbert, 1983). Fire exposes more snow to evaporation and adversely impacts water quality as runoff (Hibbert, 1983). Investments in forest health improve water quantity and water quality, with 80 years of research demonstrating its benefits for developed water supply and better water quality (Troendle, Wilcox, Bevenger, & Porth, 2001).

On the other hand, removal of vegetation can harm aquatic and wildlife habitat by reducing shade cover, eliminating key nesting areas, and increasing access to fragile banks for grazing animals (Rauscher, 1999). Furthermore, removal of the kind of scrub brush and invasive species required for better forest health and streamflow can be costly, with uncertain returns on such investments, in part because such vegetation has a narrow trunk diameter that does not lend itself well to use as timber (Bradshaw & Lueck, 2015). Burning such vegetation for energy or paper production is possible, but can result in pollution from energy production and other environmental impacts associated with brush removal (Larson, 2016).

An overview of relevant water laws and regulations in Ecuador

Ecuador was established as an independent nation in 1830, and has had 20 national constitutions since that time, with rapid normative (constitutional) change. Ecuador's current constitution was enacted in 2008, and as with past constitutions, the change was due to political influence. In the last two decades the country has had a political and ideological debate which appears in its constitutions, first with the 1998 fundamental law, under a neoliberal influence, and then with the socialist Citizens' Revolution of 2008, representing more a political document than a constitutional norm (Ayala Mora, 2015).

In 1998, the constitution served as a possible modernizing instrument in public administration, expanding the role of the private sector. Natural resources governance was restructured to benefit private enterprises, with incentives for privatization, especially public services (for example drinking water service[1]). In environmental policy, this fundamental law aimed to address the right to a healthy environment, and represented the first time that the constitution recognized access to clean water as a right, but only in relation to the right to health.

Between the 1998 neoliberal constitution and the 2008 socialist constitution, Ecuador passed through a period of serious governmental instability, with mixtures of *coups d'état*, rebellions and abandonment of power. These grave conditions allowed the presence of a 'messianic' leadership, which resulted in the rise of the Citizens' Revolution, with capital diverted to benefit the people in a model based on the principle of *sumak kawsay* (good living), an aboriginal Andean philosophy (Ávila, Grijalva, & Martínez, 2008). *Sumak kawsay* changed the development model in Ecuador, because it aims to harmonize human development with environmental protection. Another important change impacting the management of natural resources and associated with this constitutional revolution was the recognition of the rights of nature (Gudynas, 2009).

These new rights of nature and the underlying theory of *sumak kawsay* received much criticism. Ecuadorians and foreign proponents explained that this new conception of constitutional rights related to long-standing aboriginal conceptions connected to Pacha Mama (Mother Earth), in which indigenous people believe that nature is an individual goddess and the mother of all life. Therefore, under this anthropomorphic constitutional conception of water, water is legally recognized both as a human right and as a right holder (De Sousa Santos, 2010). The first case in Ecuador where this interesting concept of nature as a holder of rights was put in practice was the Vilcabamba River case involving the Loja Provincial Council (Action of Constitutional Protection). While the rights held by nature include the protection of water, the Ecuadorian constitution also incorporated a special mention for water, recognizing it as a fundamental human right (Article 3). Water is conceptualized as an essential aspect of *sumak kawsay* because access to water is essential for life, as articulated in Article 12.

If we make a chronological comparison, Ecuador's constitutional advance for their citizens with respect to water predated UN General Assembly Resolution 64/292 of 28 July 2010 recognizing an international human right to water. In 1998, Ecuador's constitution recognized the right to a healthy environment, and 10 years later, the constitution recognized natural resources, including water, as resources of strategic national importance and the subject of rights held by the public, which are inalienable and essential for life.

Under the 2008 constitution, drinking water and irrigation water services are the exclusive responsibility of the national government, because water is a part of the 'strategic sector' (Articles 313–314). The use of water is public, and its management can be public (local governments) or communal (user associations, Indigenous peoples, or rural people). Similar to the neoliberal 1998 constitution, this new constitutional text talks about the right to health (Article 32) and makes special reference to water as an essential part of good living. When the constitution talks about a decent life, drinking water is a central element (Article 66).

In Ecuador, the privatization of water sources and infrastructure is not permitted. This normative change was part of the ideological underpinnings of the 2008 political revolution against the free market and the neoliberal position of the 1998 constitution (Article 282), because that approach had allowed huge accumulation of vital water resources by private enterprises. In Ecuador, the management of water is held by the state, primarily under the executive authority of the Water Secretariat (SENAGUA) since May of 2008.

In August 2014, the Congress approved a law to regulate the use of water: the Organic Law on Water Resources, Uses, and Exploitation of Water (Water Law 2014). The country had a previously codified water law from the dictatorial period with limited public participation in private concession contracts. That law generated too much conflict for effective implementation, especially for indigenous people and social movements (Martinez Moscoso, 2015). The main objective of the new law is to guarantee the human right to water and to regulate and control water resources to secure good living (*sumak kawsay*) for all citizens. This includes a management partnership between the central government agency SENAGUA and subnational governments, including community irrigation and drinking water systems.

One of the most important results of this partnership between the central government and subnational governments is the percentage of homes with access to water. In December 2006, 69% of homes had access to drinking water, but by December 2016, it had increased to 83.6% (Consejo Nacional de Planification, 2017). However, the objective of the new law is not only focused on access to water for homes, it also refers to all activities that involve the use of this resource (integrated management).

Perhaps the principal contribution of the new law is the prioritization of water uses: (1) drinking water; (2) irrigation water (food sovereignty); (3) ecological flow; and (4) productive activities (Water Law 2014, Article 86). Also, Article 411 of the Ecuadorian constitution guarantees the conservation, restoration and integrated management of water resources at the basin level, including ecological flows and recharge zones, managed in a co-responsible partnership between the state and subnational governments, with resources and technical assistance coming from the central government.

Landowners near water sources have the obligation to comply with the regulations and technical provisions of SENAGUA to conserve and protect the water at the ecosystem and basin level in coordination with subnational governments (Water Law 2014, Article 12). The 2014 organic water law gives a list of water protection and conservation methods and approaches under Article 13, including easements for public use, water protection zones, and restriction zones. The law also prohibits forestry activities in the servient[2] area or in water protection zones (Article 100).

Water authorities and environmental authorities have the power to enact regulations and rules for the conservation of water resources and the protection and promotion of recharge zones. Importantly, SENAGUA is empowered to implement a special rate to conserve water resources and recharge zones. Subnational governments implement rates for domestic public services (drinking water) to finance these conservation and protection programmes.

The constitution of Ecuador regulates the territorial organization of watersheds. Regional governments (provinces) have exclusive competencies to manage the watersheds and promotes the creation of basin councils in accordance with the law (Article

262). The provinces have the exclusive competence to work in basins and sub-basins for the regional environmental management and to plan, build, operate and maintain irrigation systems (Article 263).

An overview of relevant water laws and regulations in Arizona

In the United States, rights to water are generally established at the state level rather than the national level. This means there is much regional variability in water rights laws. Most jurisdictions in the western US, including Arizona, base water rights on the doctrine of prior appropriation (Leshy, 2005). This doctrine is a 'first in time, first in right' regime, which allocates water to users in order of priority, limited to the amount of water that can be put to beneficial use. Under prior appropriation, when river flows are insufficient to satisfy all rights, a senior appropriator will place a 'call on the river' (Larson & Kennedy, 2016). The call forces junior appropriators to stop diverting until the senior's right is satisfied. However, under the 'futile call doctrine', a state will decline to cut off a junior appropriator if the water saved would not reach the senior user downstream – in other words, if it is futile (Larson & Kennedy, 2016). This general overview of surface water law roughly describes how water rights are allocated in Arizona (Feller, 2007).

The method used to determine water rights on federal reserved lands, like national parks or Native American lands, is different from that used for other water users. When the US reserves public land for any use, including tribal reservations, military bases, and national parks, it implicitly reserves water rights (*Arizona v. California*, 1963). These rights are called *Winters* rights, after the US Supreme Court case *Winters v. United States* (1908), which established the federally reserved water rights doctrine. The lands are reserved the minimal amount of water sufficient to meet the primary purpose for which the reservation was established (*Cappaert v. United States*, 1976). The 'primary purpose' of tribal reservations is to establish a permanent homeland (*Winters*, 1908). To quantify the amount of water necessary to achieve this purpose courts have generally used the Indian reservation's practicably irrigable acreage (*Arizona*, 1963). However, the Arizona Supreme Court refused to use the Indian practicably irrigable acreage as the only quantification method and included consideration of factors like tribal culture, population, and water use plans (In re General Adjudication of All Rights to the Gila River, 2001, discussed in Larson & Kennedy 2016). The priority date for reserved rights is time immemorial for aboriginal lands reserved, or the date the reservation was established (*United States v. Adair*, 1983, discussed in Larson & Kennedy 2016).

As western states' populations and industry continued to grow, conflicts between water users gave rise to a need for a comprehensive proceeding to determine rights (Doremus & Tarlock, 2003). Also, inter-jurisdictional competition over transboundary rivers at the sub-national level and the emergence of federally reserved rights in Native American tribes and national forests fueled the need for an integrated, basin-scale approach to the adjudication of water rights (Thorson, 1996). In 1952, Congress passed the McCarran Amendment, which waived the sovereign immunity of the US in cases determining 'rights to the use of water of a river system or other source' (Goldsby, 2011). The amendment requires adjudications to join a sufficient number of water uses – termed 'use comprehensiveness' (Benson, 2006). By allowing states to adjudicate federal water rights alongside all other appropriative rights in state courts, the amendment essentially made possible modern general stream adjudications (McElroy & Davis, 1995).

As comprehensive proceedings, general stream adjudications are lengthy, time-consuming and resource-intensive, and often span decades (Larson & Kennedy, 2016). Many western states have large comprehensive adjudications underway. One example is the Gila River Adjudication in Arizona (Feller, 2007). Begun in 1976, over 40 years later it has yet to be resolved (Larson & Kennedy, 2016). Arizona's general stream adjudication of the rights to the Gila River illustrates the nature of the proceedings and array of challenges that arise, many common among western adjudications (Larson & Kennedy, 2016).

Perhaps the greatest challenge to resolving the Gila River Adjudication is the bifurcated nature of Arizona's water rights regime (Feller, 2007). In Arizona, surface water rights are allocated according to the principles of prior appropriation described above (Larson & Kennedy, 2016). But groundwater rights are allocated differently. In densely populated regions called 'active management areas', groundwater rights are heavily regulated and dependent on grandfathered rights to limited quantities of water registered with the state agency or groundwater withdrawal permits issued by that same agency (Megdal, Nadeau, & Tom, 2011). Only surface water rights are subject to general stream adjudication process (Feller, 2007).

The legal distinction between groundwater and surface water has proved controversial and difficult to implement (Feller, 2007). Currently, Arizona law defines any subsurface water within the 'subflow' zone – meaning within the saturated floodplain Holocene alluvium – as surface water and therefore subject to general stream adjudication (Larson & Kennedy, 2016). Significant resources are devoted simply to deciding whether or not a party should be involved in the adjudication based on determining whether a well is appropriating subflow or groundwater (Larson & Kennedy, 2016).

Case studies of forestry management and water protection in Ecuador and Arizona

This section will describe two approaches to forestry management aimed at addressing water issues, one in the Paute River basin in Ecuador and the other in the Verde River basin in Arizona.

The Paute River basin in Ecuador

The Paute basin is in the south-east of Ecuador and includes three provinces: Azuay (Andean), Cañar (Andean) and Morona Santiago (Amazonian). Much of this territory was originally occupied by Cañaris Indigenous People (pre-Inca) and by the Incas (pre-colonial). These cultures had a special relationship with water, because this territory includes important water bodies that were worshiped as gods. This basin has an area of 643,923.7 hectares and is subdivided into 18 sub-basins and 75 micro-basins. One of the censuses made by SENAGUA confirms the presence of more than 460 organizations of users, totalling 83,514 users as of 2014, especially rural drinking water systems and irrigation systems. In the 1950s, the basin included only 33 such organizations.

There are important natural resources projects in the basin, including the hydro-electric project (Mazar) in south-eastern Ecuador, part of the 1,075 MW energy project called Amaluza-Molino. Approximately 50% of Ecuador's energy is generated in the Paute basin. The basin also includes the ETAPA (Empresa de Telecomunicaciones, Agua Potable, Alcantarillado y saneamiento de Cuenca) drinking water enterprise, which provides potable water and sanitation services to Cuenca, the third-largest city in Ecuador, with more than half a million users, and its rural environs. ETAPA manages its water source holistically, and is one of the principal constituents of FONAPA (Fondo del Agua para la conservación de la Cuenca del Río Paute), a cooperative aimed at protecting the watershed, including upland forests.

In 2009, Ecuador and the European Commission signed an agreement for the implementation of the project Development of the Paute River Basin, which established a master plan for the Paute River basin. Its purpose was to generate management tools to orient the activities of the basin in a sustainable way and achieve integrated development. It included a diagnostic of the situation in the basin, the conflicts and critical problems to finally propose actions, political marks and strategies to resolve these challenges and improve the quality of life of the population.

One objective of the plan is the incorporation of protected areas in the basin. The protected area in the Paute River basin corresponds to approximately 40% of its territory, of which 19% is national parks and 21% forest areas and protective vegetation. The importance of these areas lies in the close relationship between forests and water quality, as forests contribute to maintaining water quality by maximizing the purification of water in its natural environment, hence the need to keep forested areas in good condition (Hamilton, 2008).

The most important activity in the area is agriculture, but agriculture is also the main cause of water problems in the basin. For example, a recurrent case is the deficient management of the soil due to agricultural production with flood irrigation in unsuitable areas, which generates instability and erosion. The basin also faces water contamination problems due to pesticide use, runoff from livestock, and unsuitable wastewater management. The advance of the agricultural frontier has destroyed much of the *paramo* and protected forest areas (Cordero Dominguez, 2013)

REDD+ action plan: forests for good living

In 2016, the environment minister approved the REDD+ (Reducing Emissions from Deforestation and Forest Degradation in Developing Countries) Action Plan: Forests for Good Living (2016–2025) through Ministerial Resolution No. 116 (Ministerio del Ambiente 2016). Its objective is to contribute to national efforts to reduce deforestation and forest degradation through conservation, sustainable forest management, and optimization of other land uses to reduce pressure on forests, in particular upland forests like those in the Paute River basin. The REDD+ Action Plan is a set of strategic lines that point to the convergence of the country's environmental and development agendas with a territorial approach. One of these lines concentrates on forestry management for the strategic protection and enhancement of water resources.

Forests are important to guarantee the availability of water and contribute to the retention and storage functions of this resource as part of its natural cycle. They also help maintain water quality and regulate the hydrological cycle, so deforestation and forest degradation have a direct impact on water availability and quality (Ministerial Conference on the Protection of Forests in Europe, 2009). The action plan tries to reduce deforestation in the highlands to maintain the quality and quantity of the water supply.

According to Article 111 of Ecuador's 2014 Water Law, the Water Authority, in coordination with the National Environmental Authority, has to define guidelines, standards and technical tools for the protection and conservation of areas of importance for water resources, considering that the provision of water in quality and quantity is one of the environmental services of the forests.

Article 12 establishes that the Water Authority, the subnational governments, water users, community groups, and landowners who have water sources on their property are responsible for the protection, conservation and management of water sources. In this sense, the Water Funds are presented as an efficient alternative to carry out specific activities for the conservation and integrated management of water resources, adopting an ecosystem approach within the river basin system.

Investment in green infrastructure

In Latin America, most investments to ensure water (in terms of quantity and quality) to the population are made in physical or grey infrastructure, such as drinking water systems (Echevarria et al., 2015). However, in terms of cost efficiency, it is better to make investments for the conservation and/or protection of water sources (known as investment in green infrastructure), because of lower maintenance and operation costs, allowing capital investments to be postponed or reallocated (Tallis & Markham, 2012).

Given that water scarcity is both physical in terms of water access and in terms of water quality, due to the lack of adequate infrastructure investments, water management should guarantee water security in terms of quantity and quality (Echevarria et al., 2015).

In 2008, funds were established for the conservation of natural water sources in Ecuador, especially in the Cuenca-Paute region. While this has been an important investment (as discussed below), according to a 2015 study, operators of drinking water in Latin America invest less than 5% of their annual budgets in green infrastructure (Echevarria et al., 2015)

Investments in green infrastructure in Ecuador have increased since the creation of the first water fund (FONAG) in 2000. In Ecuador, it is the ETAPA EP water operator that provides potable water service (municipal and public in the city of Cuenca), and is the pioneer that led the investment in green infrastructure starting around 15 years ago, principally through FONAPA (Echevarria et al., 2015) In the 'Report on Green Infrastructure in the Drinking Water Sector in Latin America and the Caribbean: Trends, Challenges and Opportunities', it is estimated that the investment of this operator in FONAPA is approximately US$ 300,000 per year.

The general objectives of water funds are to ensure the quality and quantity of water; to ensure the regularity of the resource for the communities; to improve/maintain the water resource ecosystems; to improve the quality of life of the inhabitants; to invest in green infrastructure to save on the costs of continuous water treatment; to use sustainable financing to ensure long-term water conservation; and to use public–private multi-institutional governance (Goldman, Benitez, Calvache, & Ramos, 2010).

FONAPA water fund

The FONAPA water fund, created in October 2008 and endowed for 80 years, aims at conserving the Paute watershed in southern Ecuador.[3] The principal partners are ETAPA EP (a municipal water enterprise), the Nature Conservancy, ELECAUSTRO S.A (a public energy enterprise), CELEC (a public energy enterprise), HIDROPAUTE (a public energy enterprise), University of Cuenca, Cordillera Tropical Foundation, and EMAPAL EP (a municipal water enterprise). FONAPA is a mercantile trust, which is dedicated to raising funds for the protection of the water resource and the ecological environment of the Paute basin, including forests. Since 2014, FONAPA has incorporated two new local governments: Paute and Azogues, both within the Paute basin, in addition to Gualaceo.

FONAPA is the only fund of this type in southern Ecuador and brings together the aims of the public, private, non-governmental organizations (NGOs), and academic sectors. Three local governments have adopted ordinances to protect water resources and related forest ecosystems:

(1) Paute: local ordinance to conserve, restore and recuperate water sources, recharge groundwater and rehabilitate Paute ecosystems, as of September 2013;
(2) Gualaceo: local ordinance to conserve, restore and recuperate water sources, recharge zones, fragile ecosystems and other areas (Official Bulletin No. 294, 22 July 2014);
(3) Azogues: local ordinance to conserve, restore and recover water sources, recharge zones, fragile ecosystems and other priority areas for biodiversity protection and environmental services and natural heritage (Official Bulletin No. 294, 22 September 2014).

The areas of FONAPA's intervention include important water sources, forests, and fragile ecosystems (Ministerio del Ambiente & FONAPA, n.d.). The intervention area is the Paute River basin (644,190 ha), which is found in the provinces of Azuay, Cañar, Morona Santiago and Chimborazo. Of that area, 40,000 ha corresponds to public lands (with interventions including top-down command-and-control regulation) and 28,714 ha to private lands (with interventions conducted through reforestation and conservation partnerships). The area prioritized by the water fund amounts to 119,138 ha. Currently, there are 17 decentralized autonomous governments (between parochial, municipal, and provincial governments) comprising part of FONAPA's area of intervention by the water fund.

The Paute River basin includes three protected areas: El Cajas National Park, Sangay National Park and the Macizo del Cajas Biosphere Reserve. Also, 35% of the country's electricity is supplied from the water resources of the basin. The beneficiaries of the water fund are 800,000 people, corresponding to the population of the cities supplied by the water of the basin. While 212 families directly benefit from the interventions, due to

Table 1. FONAPA water fund intervention and beneficiaries.

Water fund	FONAPA (Fondo del Agua para la conservación de la Cuenca del Río Paute)	
Creation	2008	
Term (years)	80	
Intervention		
Intervention area (ha)	644,190	Paute River basin
Public area intervened (ha)	40,000	Control, protection and surveillance
Private area intervened (ha)	28,714	Reforestation and/or conservation
Priority area (ha)	119,138	
Provinces	4	Azuay, Cañar, Morona Santiago, Chimborazo
Regional, provincial and municipal governments	17	
Protected areas within the Paute River basin	3	El Cajas National Park, Sangay National Park, Macizo del Cajas Biosphere Reserve
Beneficiaries		
Direct	800,000	Population
Indirect	4,500,000	Population
Families benefiting directly	212	

Source: Data from Latin American Alliance of Water Funds; FONAPA, 'Plan de Implementación de Medidas y Acciones REDD+'.

the great contribution of electric power that contributes to the national level, it is estimated that 4,500,000 inhabitants benefit indirectly from the interventions (Table 1).

One of the key aspects of water funds is their financing, for which various mechanisms are available. In some cases, fixed contributions by partners are established. In the case of FONAPA, the partner's contributions are negotiated every year (Alianza Latinoamericana de Fondos de Agua [ALFA], 2017).

According to ALFA, the financial support for FONAPA is mainly constituted by public funds (almost 55%), followed by private for-profit funds (around 30%), bilateral or multilateral public–private partnerships (approximately 10%), and NGO contributions (around 5%). Approximately 90% of the increased revenue came from water funds, with the rest coming from partner contribution (ALFA, 2017).

One of the instruments used by FONAPA for the conservation of the intervention areas is the adoption of voluntary mutual agreements between the water system operator and the owners of the zones, whereby the water system operator provides incentives for the landowners to carry out environment-friendly productive livestock practices and receive payments for ecosystem services, while the operator commits to conserving water recharge areas. Other instruments used are municipal ordinances for enclosing water sources or native forests (Ministerio del Ambiente & FONAPA, n.d.).

The Verde River basin in Arizona

The Verde River begins in the ponderosa pine forests of the mountainous region of northern Arizona and flows south, where it joins the Salt River, a tributary to the Gila River, which ultimately joins the Colorado River near the US/Mexico border (Marder, 2009). It is the only river in Arizona with federal 'wild and scenic river' designation – a true ecologic and hydrogeologic gem (Marder, 2009). The Verde River, as part of the broader Gila River system, is also over-appropriated, with rights to its water under the decades-long 'general stream adjudication' process (Larson & Kennedy, 2016). One possible approach to improve the ecologic condition of the river while also increasing supplies to better meet demand involves improving the forests in which the Verde River originates.

The Four Forest Restoration Initiative (4FRI), the largest watershed management project in the US, is aimed at improving water supply by facilitating the rehabilitation of the large ponderosa pine forests in the Verde River basin (Fredette, 2016). The 4FRI effort began in 2011 and extends across four national forests. It consists of a partnership between the US Forest Service, state and tribal land management agencies, local governments, environmental protection NGOs, and public utilities (Vosick, 2016). The efforts aim to rehabilitate 2.4 million acres of forest land through forest thinning, removal of invasive species, prescribed preventive forest burns, and cooperative and adaptive 20-year management plans, with five-year review periods (Vosick, 2016).

While the initial five-year period was successful in thinning 600,000 acres, the process for environmental site assessments was frequently bogged down by litigation and accusations of lack of transparency. The costs and delays associated with maintaining a broad, collaborative group of stakeholders in the face of such litigation discouraged some integral parties from actively participating in forestry management (Vosick, 2016).

Water quality and water rights laws may also discourage stakeholder engagement. From a water quality perspective, forest thinning may result in pollutant loading from thinning activities, with such liability proving a disincentive for such activities (Oldham, 2016).

State water laws may provide further disincentives. Arizona's water law distinguishes between developed water and salvaged water (Larson, 2016). Developed water is water that was imported by humans into a basin and was not previously part of that basin – e. g., desalination or bulk water imports via tanker or pipeline. Salvaged water is water that was part of the basin but was made accessible and usable by human intervention – e.g., drilling deep into a fossil aquifer, or liberating water taken up by invasive species or other vegetation. Developed water is owned by the developing party, independent of the prior-appropriation system; salvaged water remains part of the priority system, and anyone investing in salvaging the water has no superior or special claim to that water than any other party. Water liberated through improved forestry management would almost certainly be considered salvaged water. Thus, those investing in forestry management to increase streamflows would not receive any special priority with respect to that increased supply.

Thus, the future of the Verde River's ecologic integrity, which depends on the forests, as well as the potential resolution of the general stream adjudication, which potentially depends on increased supplies in the Verde River, may require legal reforms to facilitate watershed management in the Verde's upland reaches.

What Arizona and Ecuador have to learn from each other on forests and water

The approach in Arizona's Verde River basin is more likely to succeed if it follows the path set forth by Ecuador's FONAPA in successfully encouraging broad partnerships between the public, private, NGO and academic sectors, and if it facilitates legal reforms at the local level. While the reforms suggested here do not come directly from identical governance methods in the Paute basin, they do reflect redirecting the aims of Arizona water law to more closely mirror those of FONAPA. One such reform would be to implement locally issued 'Good Samaritan permits' for forest management projects like 4FRI. These permits would authorize forest restoration and thinning projects; so long as the conditions of the permit are met, the permit would shield forestry activities from liability under environmental statutes that might otherwise discourage investment in watershed management. This sort of permitting scheme mirrors, at least in its basic aims, the voluntary agreements promoted by FONAPA to promote payments for ecosystem services.

Another possible reform to encourage greater inter-sector participation is to create regional water mitigation authorities (RWMAs). Under this approach, a mathematical model would be used to assess a well's relationship to subflow. The model would make a conservative estimate of the impact a well has on senior surface water rights, based on hydrogeologic factors. That estimate would then be used to establish a mitigation fee. The mitigation fee would be paid to an RWMA. RWMA members would voluntarily join the RWMA and pay the mitigation fee based on the model. RWMA members would then be shielded from having their rights adjudicated or subject to more senior rights, and the RWMA would be liable to make senior right holders whole through mitigation. Those who elected to remain outside the RWMA would pursue final adjudication in the general stream adjudication, including the possibility that their pumping is deemed subflow and thus subject to higher priority rights. The RWMA, on the other hand, would then take member fees and pursue ways to mitigate the impact of members' pumping on senior water rights. One potential mitigation option would be for RWMAs to finance forestry thinning to augment streamflow. This would encourage investment in forestry management projects like the 4FRI. Policy makers could further encourage this approach by reforming the concept of salvaged water, so that those investing in forestry management have heightened priority (under the prior-appropriation system) to water made available through investments in improved forests. The 4FRI project could then hold increased streamflows created through forestry management as a collectively owned and saleable water right. The challenge, however, would be the quantification of water liberated through forest management, and the concern that such reforms would encourage excessive vegetation removal, aggravating erosion and affecting streams while damaging critical habitat (Larson, 2016).

The RWMA approach might help integrate surface water and groundwater management without running afoul of the constitutional limits on recognizing subflow rights that would interfere with vested water rights in Arizona. The RWMA approach's focus on integrating surface water and groundwater, and its effort to address private property rights in water, are less relevant in Ecuador, where there are no similar vested rights to priority and where there is no subflow issue being adjudicated. Nevertheless, the RWMA reform could be adapted in the Ecuadorian context to facilitate projects like FONAPA. For example, many rural, indigenous communities in Ecuador form local water user associations, called *juntas de agua potable y saneamiento* (or simply *juntas*). These juntas could play a similar role in Ecuador as contemplated for RWMAs in Arizona. In coordination with FONAPA, they could invest in forest protection projects, resulting in juntas holding legally recognized forestry management credits. Downstream water users could purchase such credits based on a requirement by governmental permitting agencies to mitigate stream loss due to water consumption.

The replicability of FONAPA in Arizona, or of 4FRI in Ecuador, is limited by the distinct legal and hydogeologic conditions of each jurisdiction. Nevertheless, both projects have potential lessons for water management, even in places as distinct in their water challenges as the Verde Paute river basins. If a model like FONAPA is to be replicated in Arizona, or the 4FRI project is to be adapted to approximate FONAPA, it is necessary to encourage greater public engagement, for local and regional governments to institutionalize the fund, and to strengthen the presence and participation of universities to enhance research and interdisciplinary collaboration. 4FRI can do more to partner with NGOs, like FONAPA, by working with the Verde River Exchange and the Nature Conservancy to develop water offset credit markets, for example. Greater sensitivity to aboriginal conceptions of water rights among Arizona's indigenous tribes, similar to the integration of *sumak kawsay* in Ecuadorian water law, may also facilitate greater engagement by tribal interests in the 4FRI and integrate traditional ecological knowledge into the forests' management.

Perhaps the most important lesson for Arizona to draw from the FONAPA experience is the potential reimaging of the trust relationship between the state, as water steward and trustee, and its citizens, as beneficiaries. FONAPA operates as a trust for the protection of water, largely overseen by public agencies. Projects like 4FRI are unlikely to be sustainable without either top-down state mandates, or else strong incentives for continued voluntary participation. One possible approach to create strong incentives in the Verde River basin would be the establishment of a water trust comparable to FONAPA's conception (Larson & Kennedy, 2016). The state could create a trust, managed by the Department of Water Resources, into which water right holders could temporarily or permanently place claims to unused water. While in trust, those rights would be shielded from forfeiture, and would be devoted to the maintenance of in-stream ecologic flows. This would allow farmers in Arizona to benefit from improved water efficiency without the risk of losing water rights. The escrow would then serve as a clearinghouse for water rights transactions, with an expedited approval process granted by the state for all water sales conducted through the trust. The protection from forfeiture and the expedited approval process would attract buyers and sellers to the trust.

The cost to water rights buyers and sellers of relying on the trust would be that each transaction through the trust would include a hold-back of a certain percentage of the water. The hold-back would serve two purposes. First, it would create a permanent source of water rights held by the state for the protection of riparian and aquatic habitats. Second, it would ideally build up a large enough quantity of water that could be sold at a discounted rate to either RWMAs seeking to make senior water right holders whole, or to any other parties facing a loss of water supplies due to the resolution of the general stream adjudication. One of major obstacles to the resolution of the general stream adjudication is that many parties fear that the end result of the adjudication will mean the loss of their water supplies, and thus there is little incentive to seek expeditious resolution. An effective water trust, with a large enough quantity of held-back water from water transactions, might alleviate those concerns.

Nevertheless, the water trust idea in Arizona, and particularly in the Verde River basin, faces significant risks and limits. This approach may not work in a basin like the Verde River's, where there are many national and state parks and forests, and fewer large areas of irrigated land from which fallowed or retired fields could yield water placed in trust. Without enough water moving the trust, there will not be enough water held back to create a bank for stream protection and to mitigate losses from the general stream adjudication. It is also possible that merely expediting approval of water rights sales and protecting water rights from forfeiture will provide insufficient incentives, particularly given the cost of holding water back from such sales. Finally, in at least some cases, there will be a concern that the expedited approval process will violate the due process rights of senior water right holders who may be impacted by the sale of those water rights through the trust.

Adapting the FONAPA trust concept in the context of Arizona is also worthy of serious consideration. Indeed, the state of Washington in the US has relied on a similar structure to facilitate water transactions and enhance the adaptive capacity of its water rights regimes (Larson & Kennedy, 2016). Unlike FONAPA's focus on forestry protection, Washington's Trust Water Rights Program (Wash. Rev. Code § 90.42, 2014; see generally Rajnus, 2014) aims to protect salmon fisheries, so the approach would require adaptation to Arizona's legal, ecological, climatological and geographic environment (Senate and House Bill for the State of Washington 2026).

With respect to the Paute Basin and FONAPA, three possible reforms, informed in part by Arizona's approach, could improve forestry management and improve water supplies. First, in the Paute River basin, an ordinance to protect and conserve water resources and related ecosystems could provide local governments the necessary legal framework to assert more control over and better protect water resources. But if FONAPA wants to generate a large impact, it should include Cuenca in that local-level empowerment, because this city has 70% of the population of the basin. This approach would be similar to the 4FRI project in Arizona, including the Salt River Project, which provides water to much of Arizona's largest city, Phoenix. Second, the US recognition of reserved water rights held independently by tribes as sovereigns, if implemented in Ecuador, may provide greater leverage and engagement by indigenous groups in the FONAPA project, particularly for juntas, if appropriately encouraged to engage in watershed management projects. Third, FONAPA has sufficient resources to operate an independent trust to conserve water resources. But the majority of its members are public organizations, so their funds depend directly on the central administration (executive branch). Therefore, Ecuador could prioritize the use of those funds to strengthen an independent FONAPA trust shielded from executive interference.

Conclusion

Water trusts like FONAPA can play an important role in investing in green infrastructure. However, further reforms may be needed to fully actualize such investments. For example, in the case of FONAPA, there is greater funding collaboration from the public sector than the private one. This raises important questions. How to induce the private sector to participate in green infrastructure investments? Should the private sector be compelled by law (whether by taxes, permitting fees, or other mechanism) to fund green infrastructure, or should law create financial incentives to encourage voluntary investment by the private sector in green infrastructure? Facilitating green infrastructure investment like 4FRI in the Verde basin faces these same questions. Arizona can look to FONAPA for potential answers, like the participation of NGOs and the reconceptualization of the trust concept in water rights management, with water as a national strategic resource. Ecuador may look to Arizona and 4FRI, perhaps by give municipalities more power to enact protective ordinances and engage in trust management.

In the Paute River basin, citizens may resent efforts to encourage or compel green infrastructure investments as just another tax. But keeping the programme solely voluntary may limit contributions. So what is the solution? If it is mandatory, then perhaps contributors should have discretion on the amount given, above certain a minimum. If it is voluntary, greater incentives will be needed to encourage adequate contributions to fund green infrastructure projects. In the Verde River basin, the concerns are less about taxes and more that judicial or legislative measures to improve the adaptive capacity of water rights regimes will unconstitutionally interfere with vested private rights in water. This is perhaps the greatest difference in forest protection for water resource management purposes between Arizona and Ecuador – such forests and water sources are already conceived of as trust resources in Ecuador, with uniquely recognized rights based on *sumak kawsay*, but they are seen as private property with strong attendant legal protections in many instances in Arizona.

Notes

1. Guayaquil, the second largest city of Ecuador, has had a privatization contract for drinking water service with Interagua Enterprise (Veolia, France) for 30 years.
2. Servient tenement is the land over which the owner (the servient owner) grants an easement to the owner (the dominant owner) of another property (the dominant tenement). An easement is a non-possessory right to the use of another's land, for example, crossing another's land. The servient estate is the land encumbered by the easement, meaning, for example, that the servient land is the land that would be crossed.
3. It was created by CELEC to not duplicate efforts and because of its interest in hydroelectric power plants.

Acknowledgments

The authors thank the research assistance of Fanny Cabrera, economist at the Faculty of Economics and Administration of the University of Cuenca, Isabel Rodas of the Environmental Engineering Programme of the University of Cuenca, Alexander Ronchetti of Arizona State University's Sandra Day O'Connor College of Law, and the organizers and participants of the International Water Resources Association's 16th World Water Congress in Cancun, Mexico.

Disclosure statement

No potential conflict of interest was reported by the authors.

ORCID

Andrés Martínez Moscoso ⓘ http://orcid.org/0000-0002-8952-0680
Rhett Larson ⓘ http://orcid.org/0000-0001-7193-022X

References

Alianza Latinoamericana de Fondos de Agua [Latin America Alliance of Water Funds]. (2017, November. 18). *IMPACTOS - fondos de agua [IMPACTS - Water funds]*. Retrieved from http://fondosdeagua.org/esp/impactos.

Ávila, R., Grijalva, A., & Martínez, R. (2008). *Desafíos constitucionales: La Constitución Ecuatoriana del 2008 en perspectiva* [Constitutional challenges: the Ecuadorian Constitution of 2008 in perspective]. Quito: Ministerio de Justicia y Derechos Humanos (EC).

Arizona v. California. 1963. 37 U.S. 546.

Ayala Mora, E., (Ed.). (2015). *Historia constitucional* [Constitutional history]. Quito: Universidad Andina Simón Bolívar – Corporación Editora Nacional.

Benson, R. (2006). Deflating the deference myth: National interests vs. state authority under federal laws affecting water use. *Utah Law Review, 2006*, 241.

Bradshaw, K., & Lueck, D. (2015). Contracting for control of landscape – Level resources. *Iowa Law Review, 100*, 2507.

Cappaert v. United States. (1976). 426 U.S. 128.

Consejo Nacional de Planificacion [National Planning Council]. (2017). *Plan nacional del buen vivir [National plan for good living]*. Quito: SENPLADES.

Cordero Dominguez, I. (2013). *Evaluación de la gestión territorial de la cuenca del Río Paute, estrategias y líneas de acción para superarlas* [Evaluation of the territorial management of the Pautet River Basin, strategies and lines of action to overcome] (Master's thesis). Universidad de Cuenca. Retrieved from Can you add the link?

De Sousa Santos, B. (2010). *Refundación del Estado en América latina. Perspectivas desde una epistemología del Sur* [Refoundation of the state in Latin America. Perspectives from a southern epistemology]. Quito: Abya-Yala.

Doremus, H., & Tarlock, D. (2003). Fish, farms, and the clash of cultures in the Klamath Basin. *Ecology Law Quarterly, 30*, 279.

Echevarria, M., Zavala, P., Coronel, L., Montalvo, T., & Aguirre, L. M. (2015). *Infraestructura Verde en el Sector de Agua Potable en América Latina y el Caribe : Tendencias, Retos y Oportunidades* [Green infrastructure in the drinking wáter sector in Latin America and the Caribbean: Trends, Challenges, and Opportunities]. Retrieved from Forest Trends website:. https://www.forest-trends.org/publications/esp-infraestructura-verde-en-el-sector-de-agua-potable-en-america-latina-y-el-caribe/

Feller, J. (2007). The adjudication that ate Arizona water law. *Arizona Law Review, 49*, 405.

Fredette, A. (2016). 4FRI and the NEPA process. *Arizona State Law Journal, 48*, 139.

Goldman, R. L., Benitez, S., Calvache, A., & Ramos, A. (2010). *Water funds: Protecting watersheds for nature and people*, Arlington, VA: The Nature Conservancy.

Goldsby, A. (2011). The McCarran amendment and groundwater: Why Washington state should require inclusion of groundwater in general stream adjudications involving federal reserved rights. *Washington Law Review, 86*, 185.

Gudynas, E. (2009). La ecología política del giro biocentrico en la nueva Constitucion de Ecuador [The political ecology of the biocentric turn in the new Constitution of Ecuador]. *Revista de Estudios Sociales, 32*, 34.

Hamilton, L. S. (2008). *Forests and water*. Rome: Food and Agriculture Organization of the United Nations.

Hibbert, A. (1983). Water yield improvement potential by vegetation management on western rangelands. *Journal of the American Water Resources Association, 19*, 375.

Larson, R. (2016). Augmented water law. *Texas Tech Law Review, 48*, 757.

Larson, R., & Kennedy, K. (2016). Bankrupt rivers. *University of California at Davis Law Review, 49*, 1335.

Leshy, J. (2005). A conversation about takings and water rights. *Texas Law Review, 83*, 1985.

Marder, M. K. (2009). The battle to save the verde: How Arizona's water law could destroy one of the last free-flowing rivers. *Arizona Law Review, 51*, 175.

Martinez Moscoso, A. (2015). El marco jurídico de la prestación del servicio publico de agua potable y saneamineto en el Ecuador [The legal framework for the provision of the public service of drinking water and sanitation in Ecuador]. In J. Melgarejo, A. Molina, & A. Ortega Gimenez Eds., *Agua y derecho. Retos para el Siglo XXI* [Water and rights: Challenges for the 21st century] (pp. 169–189). Navarre: Aranzadi-Civitas – Thomson Reuters.

McConkey, D. (1994). Federal reserved rights to instream flows in the national forests. *Virginia Environmental Law Journal, 13*, 305.

McElroy, S., & Davis, J. (1995). Revisiting Colorado river water conservation dist. v. United States – There must be a better way. *Arizona State Law Journal, 27*, 597.

Megdal, S., Nadeau, J., & Tom, T. (2011). The forgotten sector: Arizona water law and the environment. *Arizona Journal of Environmental Law & Policy, 1*, 243.

Ministerial Conference on the Protection of Forests in Europe. (2009). *Sustainable forest management and influences of water resources*. Antalya, Turkey: European Union .

Ministerio del Ambiente & FONAPA [Ministry of the Environment & FONAPA]. (n.d.). *Plan de implementación de medidas y acciones REDD+* [REDD+ implementation plan measure and actions]. Quito: Gobierno Nacional del Ecuador o quizás Ministerio del Ambiente .

Ministerio del Ambiente [Ministry of the Environment]. (2016). *Plan de acción bosques REDD+* [REDD+ forest action plan]. Quito: Gobierno Nacional del Ecuador o quizás Ministerio del Ambiente .

Oldham, C. (2016). Wildfire liability and the federal government: A double-edged sword. *Arizona State Law Journal, 48*, 205.

Rajnus, M. (2014). Washington's water right impairment standard: How the current interpretation impedes the state's policy of maximizing net benefits. *Washington Journal of Environmental Law and Policy, 4*, 178.

Rauscher, M. (1999). Ecosystem management decision support for federal forests in the United States: A review. *Forest Ecology and Management, 114*, 173.

Senate and House Bill (S.H.B.) for the State of Washington 2026. 52nd Leg., Reg. Sess. (Wash. 1991) § 90.42.005(2)(a)

Tallis, H., & Markham, A. (2012). *Factibilidad económica de los fondos de agua: Ventajas competitivas de invertir en conservación* [Economic feasibility study of water funds: Competitive advantages of investing in conservation]. Latin America Conservation Council.

Thorson, J. (1996). *State watershed adjudications: Approaches and alternatives*. Paper presented at the 42nd Annual Rocky Mountain Mineral Law Institute, Denver, CO. 22–1, § 22.04.

Troendle, C., Wilcox, M., Bevenger, G., & Porth, L. (2001). The coon creek water yield augmentation project: Implementation of timber harvesting technology to increase streamflow. *Forest Ecology and Management, 143*, 179.

United Nations General Assembly. (2010). The human right to water and sanitation. A/RES/64/292. United Nations.

Vosick, D. (2016). Democratizing federal forest management through public participation and collaboration. *Arizona State Law Journal, 48*, 93.

Water Law. (2014). *Ley Orgánica de Recursos Hídricos, Uso y Aprovechamiento del Agua*. Quito: Asamblea Nacional del Ecuador.

Winters v. United States. (1908). 207 U.S. 564.

Factors identifying aquifers with a high probability of management success

Eric L. Garner ⓘ

Introduction

There is a great deal of scientific evidence documenting groundwater overuse around the world. Despite this evidence, many and perhaps most aquifers are not managed sustainably. In California, for example, significant overdraft issues have been well known for a long time, yet overdraft of aquifers throughout the state continues, most notably in the state's central region. In southern California, however, there is a cluster of aquifers that are being managed with great success. California's contrasting examples raise the question of how aquifers that have so much in common – including climate, economy and legal system – can experience such different results in the pursuit of sustainable management. This paper hypothesizes that understanding the differences between aquifers where management has and has not succeeded inside and outside of California will provide key information for improving the effectiveness of aquifer management efforts worldwide.

To this end, this viewpoint examines the following aquifers that are successfully managed or have taken important steps towards management: the Genevese Aquifer in France and Switzerland, the Los Sotillos Aquifer in Spain, the Eastern Snake Plain Aquifer in the US state of Idaho, and a number of California basins governed by a court-ordered 'physical solution'. These aquifers are contrasted with others that continue to be overused, including the Central Valley Basin in California, the Ogallala Aquifer in the Midwestern United States and the Sana'a Aquifer in Yemen. The paper also notes the Guarani Aquifer in Argentina, Brazil, Paraguay and Uruguay, where Paraguay recently became the fourth and final state to ratify a transboundary agreement for aquifer management, and yet implementation of the agreement has not yet begun and overuse of the aquifer continues.

Where groundwater management is accomplished, the following factors have been integral to success: (1) an imminent, certain and broad threat of long-term damage to the water supply; (2) the presence of urban water users; (3) a source of supplemental water; (4) the presence of junior water rights holders; (5) a relatively small aquifer; and (6) a 'bottom-up' solution developed by aquifer users coupled with existing structures to facilitate 'top-down' enforcement if needed. This paper expands upon each factor with examples from the surveyed basins.

The California groundwater experience

In California, unregulated groundwater extraction supplies 41% of the water needs of a large and growing urban population and 39% of the irrigation for a US$46 billion agricultural industry. While California passed its first groundwater legislation in 2014, implementation of the Sustainable Groundwater Management Act (SGMA) is just beginning. It is still unclear how SGMA, which imposes local sustainability planning requirements, not a state-wide regulatory scheme, will impact pumping. For this reason, it is not addressed further in this paper.

California aquifers have all the elements of Hardin's tragedy of the commons.[1] Pumping is not regulated, the pool of groundwater users continues growing, surface water supplies are highly variable, the relatively dry Mediterranean climate is excellent for agriculture and imported water is expensive. Economist Elinor Ostrom has written that, as a result of these factors, 'over extraction was the logical outcome' in California (Ostrom, 1990, p. 106). It is certainly not surprising then that California's Central Valley has been one of the world's most publicized examples of an overdrafted and unmanaged aquifer. What is much less publicized is that California has also produced enduring aquifer management successes stories.

California has a process for creating, implementing and maintaining sustainable groundwater management institutions that is neither quick nor inexpensive, but has worked, and its principles are applicable anywhere. The process is usually initiated when groundwater users seek a legal adjudication of the aquifer and culminates with the installation of a 'watermaster', usually an engineer or a local political entity, which oversees groundwater use and aquifer management according to the terms of a physical solution under the supervision of a court (Garner, 2014, 2016). While most of California's aquifers remain unmanaged, 27 of its basins are governed by physical solutions today.[2] Some of these physical solutions have been in place for over 40 years, and many have been very successful at sustainably managing their aquifers. By comparing these managed basins with the many that are not, it is possible to isolate general factors that are present in the managed basins and that likely contribute to their successes. This is true outside of California as well.

Certain, imminent and broad threats

Something must be the catalyst for the management process to begin. In aquifers that have instituted successful management systems, the process is usually started by a threat to the continued use of the aquifer that is certain, imminent and broad. This means that there is general agreement about the existence of the threat, it is likely to impact water users in the near term and the threat includes most, if not all, of the users in the basin.

Significantly, evidence of groundwater overdraft on its own often fails to drive management implementation. In fact, groundwater users have a long history of ignoring or challenging evidence of overdraft (Ostrom, 1964). Despite technological advancements, including data collected by the satellite missions Gravity Recovery and Climate

Experiment (GRACE) and Landstat, that have made evidence of overdraft, declining groundwater levels and groundwater use more accurate and accessible than ever before, groundwater users throughout the world continue to pump from overdrafted aquifers that are in serious trouble. In a 2016 survey of California groundwater users performed by Stanford University's Water in the West Program, only 31% of respondents reported using satellite data, 36% indicated they did not have data sets or had highly uncertain data sets for sustainable yield, and nearly 60% did not feel they had adequate ground-water level data for decision-making purposes (Moran, Cravens, Martinez, & Szeptycki, 2016). A similar lack of stakeholder engagement with available scientific evidence has been noted in the Guarani Aquifer (Foster, Kemper, Garduño, Hirata, & Nanni, 2006). A key reason for this is that in most areas groundwater is the least expensive source of water and no one wants to reduce the amount of water they are pumping.

Groundwater users' continued scepticism about overdraft also may be in part because of the complicated relationship aquifers have with both interconnected surface water and changing climate conditions (Jacobs et al., 2009). In fact, even where evidence of overdraft is indisputable, scientists acknowledge that their understanding of the remaining groundwater supply is still quite limited (Famiglietti, 2014).

Furthermore, even extreme examples of overdraft may not be an immediate threat to groundwater availability in the short term. This is particularly true for large aquifers. In the mid-United States, the Ogallala Aquifer underlies more than 47,750 km^2 and parts of eight states. Since predevelopment, storage in the Ogallala Aquifer has been depleted by approximately 330 km^3, an amount that scientists predict would take 6000 years to refill by natural processes (Finley, 2017; Little, 2009). Groundwater declines within the aquifer have been measured at up to 75 m. Between 2003 and 2013, overdraft continued at an average rate of 12.5 km^3 per year (Famiglietti, 2014). Yet, as of 2013, 3601 km^3 of water remained in the aquifer (McGuire, 2014). Similarly, in the Central Valley of California, aquifer storage was depleted by 71 km^3 between 1962 and 2003, resulting in groundwater level declines in some areas of more than 120 m. Nonetheless, nearly 1000 km^3 of water remains within pumping range in the upper 300 m of the aquifer (Faunt, 2009). Projections for how long these aquifers can continue to meet demand vary, but generally fall within the range of 100 years. Ongoing advancements in pumping technology have the potential to reach deeper water, stretching projections even further into the future.

In contrast to overdraft alone, the threat of saltwater intrusion has led to a number of aquifers being successfully managed. Once declining groundwater levels approach sea level, saltwater intrusion presents a threat that is both imminent and broad. A relatively small drop in the groundwater level can lead to widespread contamination. Once contaminated, wells must be closed or require expensive treatment. Perhaps because of its potential to impact all users and the immediacy of the threat, reports of saltwater intrusion generally have not been met with the same scepticism applied to evidence of overdraft and are more readily accepted as scientific certainty.

In the West Coast Basin of Los Angeles, California, declining groundwater levels were first reported around 1900. The report went largely ignored and, in the decades that followed, groundwater use steadily increased as the deep turbine pump was introduced to the area, industry took root and the urban population grew. In the 1920s, some groundwater users began noticing that water levels in their wells were approaching sea level. By the 1930s, coastal wells began showing evidence of saltwater intrusion. Nonetheless, groundwater users throughout the basin continued to look at these instances as isolated, local problems. Various attempts by impacted groundwater users to address saltwater intrusion failed to attract enough participation from aquifer pumpers for management to occur. The turning point for initiating management came in 1944 when the US Geological Survey issued a report that demonstrated the potential for saltwater intrusion to extend across the entire aquifer. For the first time, a critical mass of groundwater producers believed there was a problem that required cooperation to resolve, and efforts to manage the basin began in earnest (Ostrom, 1964). Citing similar histories in other California basins, including Orange County Basin and Seaside Basin, scholars have acknowledged that saltwater intrusion is often the initial motivator of successful management efforts in California (Langridge, Brown, Rudestam, & Conrad, 2016; Leahy, 2016; Ostrom, 1964).

Other threats that have led to management include arsenic contamination, damaged infrastructure and depleted connected surface water resources. Each of these threats can be demonstrated with certainty and has the potential to impact all users.

Urban water suppliers

Instituting groundwater management anywhere is an expensive and time-consuming process, from the initial hydrologic analysis of the aquifer to determining pumping allocations, acquiring supplemental water, operating and maintaining infrastructure, and continuing oversight of water use and aquifer conditions. The cost, particularly for small pumpers, usually will not justify the expenditure. The financial equation is different, however, for urban water suppliers. Urban water suppliers have long-term interests in sustainable local water supplies – they cannot close or take their business elsewhere and they are often specifically charged with planning for future supplies. In addition, they can pass the cost on to a pool of rate payers, thereby limiting the impact on any individual user. Moreover, urban water suppliers are generally governed by elected bodies responsible to the public and thus subject to public pressure. As a result, urban water suppliers have funded groundwater management all over the world. Examples include most adjudicated California basins and the Genevese Aquifer in France and Switzerland (de Los Cobos, 2018).

In contrast, in California's Central Valley, where there has been significant overdraft and virtually no management, agricultural pumpers are responsible for approximately 85% of groundwater extracted. A large percentage of the remaining 15% is pumped by private wells for domestic use. In fact, public supply wells account for just 4670 of the 236,115 wells in the Central Valley (California Department of Water Resources, 2015). For this reason, urban water suppliers have not been able to fund the large-scale efforts required to manage the Central Valley's basins sustainably, and farming interests have not acted.

Availability of supplemental water

In an overdrafted aquifer, some combination of reduced pumping and increased recharge is required to bring the basin into balance. Increased recharge, however, requires a supplemental water source. Although supplemental water is expensive, without it, pumping must be reduced to native safe yield. A dramatic pumping reduction has such a significant impact on all basin users that it is often not a viable option.

In southern California, supplemental water has largely been supplied by the Metropolitan Water District, a regional water wholesaler formed in 1928 for the express purpose of supplementing local supplies. The physical solutions that govern adjudicated southern California aquifers typically direct pumpers to purchase Metropolitan Water District or other supplemental water to offset groundwater use and recharge the basin. As a result, a number of southern California basins have been able to be sustainably managed while continuing to have production that exceeds, sometimes substantially, native safe yield.

In the Genevese Aquifer of France and Switzerland, an overdraft of 7 million m^3 per year was eliminated with the construction of a single recharge plant in 1980 using treated water from the Arve River. While an initial pumping reduction was required to return groundwater to historical levels, extractions now regularly exceed pre-recharge levels without causing overdraft (de Los Cobos, 2018; Wohlwend, 2002).

In contrast, in California's Central Valley, available water imports are already allocated to existing uses, yet eliminating overdraft in the Central Valley's basins with pumping reductions alone could cost an estimated US$1 billion annually in lost agricultural production (Nelson et al., 2016). This cost and the lack of an additional supplemental water source to offset it are major challenges to achieving sustainable aquifer management in the Central Valley.

Junior water rights holders

Junior water rights holders are often the first to seek groundwater management because their pumping rights are at risk of reduction in times of shortage. When faced with the risk of losing their pumping rights all together, junior water rights holders generally seek compromise in exchange for a more certain groundwater allocation. In contrast, senior water rights holders typically advocate for maintaining the status quo and strict priority because they believe they can exclude others from pumping (or require monetary payment from them) before being compelled to reduce their own use. It is often not until the senior water rights holders are at the point where they have to prove their water usage that they are willing to compromise.

In Idaho's Eastern Snake Plain Aquifer, all groundwater pumpers have water rights that are junior to surface water rights along the hydrologically connected Snake River. When overdraft of the aquifer reduces river flows, right holders on the river can call for curtailment of groundwater uses. Beginning in the 1990s, curtailment calls were made with regularity. In 2015, groundwater pumpers agreed voluntarily to reduce withdrawals by 300 million m^3 per year and to fund the purchase of replacement water in exchange for safe harbour from curtailment orders (Idaho Department of Water Resources, 2016; Idaho Water Resources Board, 2009; Matthews, 2016).

In California, urban water suppliers are often among the most junior water rights holders in a basin, while groundwater users who pump and use water on their overlying land for agricultural or domestic purposes generally hold the highest priority water rights. This is another reason why urban water suppliers have taken leading roles in creating and funding management institutions in California (Ostrom, 1964).

In the Central Valley, most wells are operated by overlying landowners who share senior rights to aquifer production. Their pumping has never been restricted, even during the 2012–16 drought when California, for the first time, curtailed the exercise of appropriative surface water rights. There has been no reason for these aquifer users to submit voluntarily to a system that would reduce their water use or charge them for aquifer management.

Aquifer size

In a smaller aquifer, it is easier to gather data, engage stakeholders and enforce a management agreement. In addition, stakeholders are more likely to have things in common, including culture, language, water uses and the impact of overdraft.

The Los Sotillos Aquifer in Andalucía, Spain, benefitted from few of the factors presented in this paper. Nonetheless, the small aquifer with 21 agricultural users has been sustainably managed since 1987. The users cooperatively created rules and a management institution with technical support from a hydrogeologist who knew the region and had the support of the community. Today, a Community of Irrigators assigns users with an equal allocation per hectare each year based on aquifer conditions (Fernandez, 2017).

In contrast, aquifers such as Central Valley, Ogallala and the Guarani Aquifer in South America support millions of users and a variety of uses over vast areas of land. Ogallala spans eight states, each with its own water rights laws, while Guarani spans four countries. In these large aquifers a pumper's extraction draws water from a broad area causing only marginal impacts to the pumper's own water levels. In fact, the worst impacts of pumping may not be felt in the area where the most pumping occurs, but rather along the edges of the aquifer.

Bottom up and top down

Sustainable aquifer management is unique in each basin and definitely is not a 'one-size -fits-all' proposition. The most enduring management structures are developed locally by the water users themselves while taking into careful consideration the specific characteristics of the aquifer. Since they have developed it, this 'bottom-up' approach frequently gives the users a vested interest in the success of the management structure. However, such an approach often needs a 'top-down' enforcement mechanism to be successful. Thus, ideally, after the management structure is instituted, there is then a system in place to enforce compliance from above.

That is the case in California, where physical solutions are generally developed by agreement of the groundwater users, but a court maintains continuing jurisdiction to enforce the physical solution as needed. The California adjudication process typically proceeds as follows: a lawsuit is filed that brings all users of an aquifer together; technical analysis of the basin is performed to determine its safe yield; negotiations and/or a trial leads to an allocation of the right to use water from the basin; a fee is set and charged for pumping in excess of one's allocation; supplemental water is secured, often with funds raised from fees, to recharge the basin; an adaptive management structure is created and vested with authority; and a court maintains continuing jurisdiction over the parties to enforce the physical solution and resolve disputes. Usually, most of these steps are crafted and carried out by agreement of a majority of aquifer users. The resulting management structures have been, in comparison with most other basins, remarkably successful. In fact, California's 2014 Sustainable Groundwater Management Act explicitly exempts these adjudicated basins by name from its sustainability planning requirements.

In Spain's Los Sotillos Aquifer, the groundwater users similarly created a management regime using technical data and cooperation. The Community of Irrigators that allocates groundwater use in the basin is mostly self-sufficient thanks to the strength of the user's participation and buy-in. However, the community reports to the river basin district authorities which can provide both oversight and support.

A number of basins have tried a purely top-down approach to groundwater management. The Sana'a Aquifer in Yemen offers a cautionary tale for this approach to groundwater management. The aquifer underlies 320,000 ha and has a population of nearly 3 million people. Most of the water produced is used to irrigate agriculture (80%); the rest is used by the urban population (Foster, 2003; RTI International, 2011). Between 2003 and 2010, the World Bank conducted a US$33 million aquifer management project in the basin. As part of the project, it established a water user's association and charged the association with implementing and enforcing a regulatory structure that prohibited activities such as well drilling without a licence (IEG, 2012). At the project's completion, the World Bank's Independent Evaluation Group (IEG) determined that the legal and regulatory framework was ineffective and rated the project 'moderately unsatisfactory'. During the project's period, 614 illegal wells were drilled compared with 106 licensed wells. The IEG concluded that '[a]n approach involving greater reliance on community-based governance, backed by technical assistance and an adequate legal framework, may have been more successful than the top-down regulatory one adopted, but was not considered' (IEG, 2012, p. 10).

Conclusions

Implementing effective groundwater management, from the initial engagement of water users to the funding and establishment of management institutions, is a very difficult process in any basin. Despite this, the presence of any number of the following factors may facilitate the process: (1) a threat of long-term damage to the water supply that is imminent, certain and broad; (2) urban water users who are reliant on a long-term sustainable supply; (3) a source of supplemental water; (4) junior water rights holders; (5) a relatively small aquifer; and (6) local engagement coupled with the availability of 'top-down' enforcement mechanisms. These factors can be leveraged, based on the lessons of prior successes and failures, to engage water users, develop mutually beneficial compromises and bolster management institutions. At a time when the number of aquifers under great stress exceeds the resources available to develop sustainable solutions, these factors also can be used to prioritize aquifers that are most likely to benefit from an investment in management implementation.

Disclosure statement

No potential conflict of interest was reported by the author.

Notes

1. Using the analogy of a common pasture, Garrett Hardin wrote that when access to a limited resource is open and unregulated, rational resource users are destined to deplete it: 'Adding together the component partial utilities, the rational herdsman concludes that the only sensible course for him to pursue is to add another animal to his herd. And another; and another. [...] Each man is locked into a system that compels him to increase his herd without limit – in a world that is limited. Ruin is the destination towards which all men rush, each pursuing his own best interest [...].' (Hardin, 1968, p. 1244).
2. California has an estimated 515 groundwater basins, 127 of which have been identified as important groundwater resources (California Department of Water Resources, 2015).

ORCID

Eric L. Garner ⓘ http://orcid.org/0000-0002-8508-9686

References

California Department of Water Resources. (2015). *California's groundwater update 2013: A compilation of enhanced content for California water plan update 2013*. Retrieved from http://www.water.ca.gov/waterplan/topics/groundwater/index.cfm

de Los Cobos, G. (2018).The Genevese transboundary aquifer (Switzerland–France): The secret of 40 years of successful management. *Journal of Hydrology: Regional Studies*, undefined, undefined. Retrieved from https://www.sciencedirect.com/science/article/pii/S2214581817302665?via%3Dihub

Famiglietti, J. S. (2014). The global groundwater crisis. *Nature Climate Change, 4*, 945–948.

Faunt, C. C., ed. (2009). Groundwater availability of the central Valley Aquifer, California. *U.S. Geological Survey Professional Paper 1766*. Retrieved from https://pubs.usgs.gov/pp/1766/

Fernandez, J. M. (2017, March). *Groundwater management in Los Sotillos community*. Presentation given at World Bank Water Regional Workshop: Groundwater Resources Management in the Mediterranean, Marseille, France.

Finley, B. (2017, October). The water under Colorado's Eastern Plains is running dry as farmers keep irrigating "great American desert." *Denver Post*. Retrieved from http://www.denverpost.com/2017/10/08/colorado-eastern-plains-groundwater-running-dry/

Foster, S. (2003). Yemen: Rationalizing groundwater resource utilization in the Sana'a basin. World Bank *GW•MATE Case Profile Collection Number 3, revised*. Retrieved from http://siteresources.worldbank.org/INTWRD/Resources/GWMATE_English_CP_02.pdf.

Foster, S., Kemper, K., Garduño, H., Hirata, R., & Nanni, M. (2006). The Guarani Aquifer initiative for transboundary groundwater management. *World Bank GW•MATE Case Profile Collection Number 9, revised*. Retrieved from http://siteresources.worldbank.org/INTWRD/Resources/GWMATE_English_CP9.pdf

Garner, E. L. (2014). Water scarcity: A role for reasonableness and physical solution in water law in an era of climate change. *Bloomberg BNA Water Law & Policy Monitor, 2014*(9).

Garner, E. L. (2016). Adapting water laws to increasing demand and a changing climate. *Water International, 41*(6), 883–899.

Hardin, G. (1968). The tragedy of the commons. *Science, 162*, 1243–1248.

Idaho Department of Water Resources. (2016). *IDWR issues curtailment order to approximately 160 junior ground water users in Eastern Snake Plain Aquifer area; juniors must join mitigation plans or face shutoff* (News Release No. 2016-10). Retrieved from https://idwr.idaho.gov/files/news-release/20160518-news-release-2016-10.pdf

Idaho Water Resources Board (2009). *Eastern Snake Plain Aquifer (ESPA) Comprehensive aquifer management plan.* Retrieved from http://www.idwr.idaho.gov/waterboard/WaterPlanning/CAMP/ESPA/PDFs/ESPA_CAMP_lowres.pdf

Independent Evaluation Group. (2012). *ICR review: Sana'a Basin water management project* (Report No. ICRR 13585). Retrieved from http://documents.worldbank.org/curated/en/568711474484799914/pdf/000020051-20140624193603.pdf

Jacobs, K., Lebel, L., Buizer, J., Addams, L., Matson, P., McCullough, E., ... Finan, T. (2009). Linking knowledge with action in the pursuit of sustainable water-resources management. *Proceedings of the National Academy of Sciences of the United States of America, 113*(17), 4591–4596.

Langridge, R., Brown, A., Rudestam, K., & Conrad, E. (2016). *An evaluation of California's adjudicated groundwater basins.* California State Water Resources Control Board. Retrieved from https://www.waterboards.ca.gov/water_issues/programs/gmp/docs/resources/swrcb_012816.pdf.

Leahy, T. C. (2016). Desperate times call for sensible measures: The making of the California sustainable groundwater management act. *Golden Gate University Environmental Law Journal, 9*(1), 4. Retrieved from http://digitalcommons.law.ggu.edu/gguelj/vol9/iss1/4

Little, J. B. (2009, March). The Ogallala Aquifer: Saving a vital U.S. Water source. *Scientific American.* Retrieved from https://www.scientificamerican.com/article/the-ogallala-aquifer/

Matthews, M. (2016, January). Groundwater pumpers prepare to pay price for historic water deal. *Magic Valley.* Retrieved from http://magicvalley.com/business/agriculture/groundwater-pumpers-prepare-to-pay-price-for-historic-water-deal/article_fe335771-7d12-5778-adc4-41d3b28e4a8b.html

McGuire, V. L. (2014). *Water-level changes and change in storage in the High Plains aquifer, predevelopment to 2013 and 2011–13* (Scientific Investigations Report No. 2014-5218). Reston, Virginia: U.S. Department of the Interior & U.S. Geological Survey. doi:10.3133/sir20145218

Moran, T., Cravens, A., Martinez, J., & Szeptycki, L. (2016). *From the ground down: Understanding local groundwater data collection and sharing practices in California.* Stanford University: Water in the West. Retrieved from http://waterinthewest.stanford.edu/sites/default/files/GW-DataSurveyReport.pdf

Nelson, T., Chou, H., Zikalala, P., Lund, J., Hui, R., & Medellín-Azuara, J. (2016). Economic and water supply effects of ending groundwater overdraft in California's Central Valley. *San Francisco Estuary & Watershed Science, 14*(1). doi:10.15447/sfews.2016v14iss1art7

Ostrom, E. (1964). *Public entrepreneurship: A case study in ground water basin management* (Unpublished PhD dissertation). University of California, Los Angeles, California.

Ostrom, E. (1990). *Governing the commons: The evolution of institutions for collective action.* New York, NY: Cambridge University Press.

RTI International. (2011). *The Sana'a water issues and options study* (Draft Final Report). Prepared for review by the World Bank.

Wohlwend, B. (2002). An overview of groundwater in international law: A case study: The Franco-Swiss Genevese Aquifer. Paper prepared for Workshop III on 'Harmonization of Diverging Interests in the Use of Shared Water Resources' in Beirut, Lebanon, organized by the United Nations Economic and Social Commission for Western Asian & German Technical Cooperation.

The evolving framework for transboundary cooperation in the Nubian Sandstone Aquifer System

Elena Quadri

ABSTRACT

The focus of this paper is the Nubian Sandstone Aquifer System, shared by Egypt, Chad, Sudan and Libya, and the agreements and other instruments of cooperation in place among the four countries. These combined instruments bear witness to an evolutionary pattern of cooperation, centred on procedural norms and on a joint institution. In the author's opinion, the four countries should strive to attain a more mature level of cooperation covering substantive norms and the settlement of disputes. The author recommends the UN Draft Articles on the Law of Transboundary Aquifers (2008) as a basis for such an agreement.

Introduction

The importance of protecting transboundary aquifers from over-exploitation and from pollution, and the importance of cooperation to this end among the countries concerned, must not be under-estimated (Stephan, 2009). State practice in the matter is evolving, as shown by the handful of inter-state agreements on record. These agreements address the Genevese Aquifer (concluded by the French and the Swiss local authorities in 1978 and replaced by the Convention on the Protection, Utilization, Recharge and Monitoring of the Franco-Swiss Genevois Aquifer in 2007), the North-Western Sahara Aquifer System (memoranda of understanding of 2002 and 2008 among Algeria, Libya and Tunisia), the Guarani Aquifer System (2010 agreement among Argentina, Brazil, Paraguay and Uruguay), the Nubian Sandstone Aquifer System (Joint Authority Agreement by Egypt, Libya in 1992 – Sudan joined in 1996 and Chad in 1999 – and Agreements 1 and 2 by Egypt, Libya, Sudan and Chad in 2000), and the Iullemeden Aquifer System (memorandum of understanding [MOU] of 2009 among Mali, Niger and Nigeria for the establishment of a trilateral consultative arrangement). The Iullemeden Aquifer System MOU is not yet in force and is to be replaced by a later agreement, the Iullemeden and Taoudeni/Tanezrouft Aquifer Systems (ITAS) MOU, made in 2014 by Algeria, Benin, Burkina Faso, Mali, Mauritania, Niger and Nigeria for the establishment of a comparable multipartite consultative mechanism for the ITAS. This later MOU is likewise not yet in effect pending the signature of three of the parties (Burchi, 2018). These agreements bear out an evolutionary pattern of cooperation, resting on the apparent will of the aquifer states to engage in increasing levels and intensity of collaboration primarily on procedural grounds, since only procedural rules relating to the exchange of data/information and the monitoring of the aquifer emerge from the agreements put in place.

This paper focusses on the Nubian Sandstone Aquifer System (NSAS), and on the substantive and procedural rules of inter-state behaviour adopted by the NSAS states through agreements made since 1992. The NSAS is the largest known fossil aquifer in the world, home to one of the largest reserves of non-recharging groundwater (Margat, Foster, & Droubi, 2006; Thorweihe, 1990). The aquifer lies in the eastern part of the Sahara. It consists of two large basins: the Nubian Sandstone Aquifer, which is the more ancient and the larger of the two and straddles the political boundaries of four north-eastern African states – Chad, Egypt, Libya and Sudan – and the more recent Post-Nubian Aquifer, which underlies only Egypt and Libya (Salem & Pallas, 2002). The NSAS extends over 2.2 million km^2; 373,000 km^2 (17.1%) lies in north-western Sudan, 233,000 km^2 (10.7%) in north-eastern Chad, 754,000 km^2 (34.7%) in south-eastern Libya, and 816,000 km^2 (37.5%, the larget share) in Egypt (Bakhbakhi, 2006). Estimates of groundwater storage vary, with estimate of 457,570 km^3 by the Centre for Environment and Development for the Arab Region and Europe (CEDARE) reckoned to be the most accurate and reliable (Bakhbakhi, 2006). Water quality varies, from excellent in the southern reaches of the aquifer to very salty in the northern reaches, in Libya (Alker, 2008). Exploitation of this enormous freshwater reserve has been on the rise in the past 40 years, with nearly 40 km^3 extracted by Egypt and Libya, mainly for irrigation and drinking water supply projects.

Agreements among Chad, Egypt, Libya and Sudan bearing out cooperation on the Nubian Sandstone Aquifer System

The Joint Authority for the Study and Development of NSAS (1992)

The agreements progressively made by Chad, Egypt, Libya and Sudan attest to the slow yet steady cooperation process among the four countries. Cooperation between Egypt and Libya, the two main users of the aquifer, had begun already in the seventies (CEDARE, 2014). In the desert areas far from the Nile, the aquifer is the only source of water for drinking, irrigation, livestock and industry. Safeguarding the aquifer from over-exploitation and from pollution is therefore a sheer necessity, and monitoring cross-border impacts from groundwater extraction is of prime importance to maintain good neighbourly relations in the region. Egypt and Libya thus recognized early on the advantages of joint management of the aquifer, through the study and sharing of knowledge and experience with a view to developing a regional strategy for the exploitation and use of the aquifer and its resources (CEDARE, 2014). This mounting awareness crystallized eventually in the establishment by the two countries of the Joint Authority for the Study and Development of NSAS (the Authority), on 29 June 1991. Sudan joined the Authority on 18 April 1996, and Chad on 18 March 1999. The use of NSAS groundwater by the two latter countries, however, is currently limited to with-drawals by the native populations of the overlying oases (Regional Strategic Action Programme for the Nubian Aquifer System, 2013). The agreement regarding the Authority is the first step in the process of cooperation among the parties. However, the only instrument on record regarding the Authority is an agreement setting forth the internal structure, functions, decision-making process, and funding of the Authority.[1] The agreement carries no provisions, substantive or procedural, regarding the management of the aquifer or of the groundwater stored in it.

As regards the internal structure of the Authority, a board manages the Authority. Each member state appoints three members to the board (Article 5). The Authority has an administrative secretariat and technical, administrative, legal and other staff. The most prominent functions of the Authority are found in Article 3:

- to collect and study information and data;
- to prepare and execute studies regarding the NSAS;
- to develop programmes, plans, and a common policy, regarding the utilization of the aquifer water;
- to study the environmental aspects of the development of groundwater stored in the aquifer, including desertification control;
- to promote the rationing of NSAS groundwater consumption in the member states.

There are national offices of the Authority in each member country. They can liaise with the Authority and provide it with information and data. They can also foster the exchange of personnel and the sharing of experience with other transboundary water commissions. The financial resources of the Authority consist of annual contributions by the member states and donations from national and international institutions, organizations, and donor states (Article 21). In particular, Egypt and Libya contribute 35% of the budget, Sudan 20%, and Chad 10% (Mirghani, 2012). The joint authority agreement makes no provision regarding the legal status of the Authority, or the settlement of disputes (Burchi & Spreij, 2003).

Agreements on monitoring and information exchange (2000)

Two agreements, both made in Tripoli on 5 October 2000 and primarily setting forth procedural-type rules, marked a significant advance in the process of cooperation among the NSAS states. The agreements, which were brokered by CEDARE (2002), sprang from the conviction that constant monitoring and updating of data and information regarding the NSAS, and sharing of these data and information, are at the heart of the sustainable use of groundwater resources in the aquifer. Agreement No.1 sets forth 'Terms of Reference for the Monitoring and Exchange of Groundwater Information of the Nubian Sandstone Aquifer System' (see the Appendix). Agreement No.2 provides 'Terms of Reference for Monitoring and Data Sharing' (see the Appendix). In the former, the four countries agreed to share the data which had been collected and systematized through the Programme for the Development of a Regional Strategy for the Utilization of the NSAS. In the latter, the countries acknowledged the need for continued monitoring of the aquifer, and for sharing of the results, with a view to the sustainable development and management of the aquifer.

Regional Action Programme for the Integrated NSAS Management (2006)

Another important step in the process of cooperation among the four NSAS countries is the Regional Action Programme for the Integrated NSAS Management, funded by the Global Environment Facility (GEF) and implemented by the United Nations Development Programme (UNDP), International Atomic Energy Agency (IAEA), and UNESCO-IHP (Regional Action Programme for the Integrated NSAS Management – Medium Sized Project, 2006). The programme supports the development of a regional strategy for integrated NSAS management, aimed at the exploitation of the aquifer in the long term and the satisfaction of the water needs of the four aquifer countries. It fosters a better understanding of aquifer issues and of potential responses, while at the same time laying the foundations for a regional Strategic Action Plan (SAP). In particular, the long-term goal of the programme is to achieve 'equitable and reasonable' management of the aquifer, for socio-economic development and for the protection of biodiversity and of natural resources. Four discrete objectives support the achievement of the over-arching programme goals:

- the identification of priority transboundary threats and their root causes, addressed in a Shared Aquifer Diagnostic Analysis (SADA, 2016). The SADA has pointed to population growth, inadequate governance structures at the regional and national levels, and poverty as the primary causes of the threats to the aquifer;
- filling gaps in data and capacity through appropriate technical approaches, necessary to make strategic planning decisions;
- preparation of an SAP delineating the policy, institutional and legal reforms which will be required to deal with the threats and their causes identified in the SADA; and
- an institutional structure for the implementation of the SAP.

A legal and institutional framework is envisaged, centred on an NSAS convention for the management and rational use of the aquifer and backed jointly by all four aquifer countries.

The Regional Strategic Action Plan for the NSAS (2013)

The Regional SAP for the joint management of the NSAS was signed by the four aquifer countries and the Joint Authority in Vienna on 18 September 2013 (Regional Strategic Action Programme for the Nubian Aquifer System, 2013). The plan commits the countries to implement actions for the sustainable management of the aquifer, based on the findings of the SADA. Three main objectives emerge from a careful reading of the SAP:

(1) To strengthen the role and capacity of the Joint Authority in the management of the shared aquifer. In particular, trans-national mechanisms are envisaged, aimed at strengthening cooperation through the Authority, and at opening up new areas of cooperation, notably as regards capacity building. A complementary line of action is the development of a regional policy inclusive of ecosystem monitoring and management, as part of the Authority's responsibilities. The Authority is thus expected to engage in regional policy making, and in the legal and institutional aspects of the NSAS (Elbadawy, 2014).
(2) To update the existing aquifer monitoring and data exchange arrangements, with a view to improved data management.
(3) To improve the effectiveness of the Authority's national offices.

In an effort to encourage efficient use of water resources, and to minimize the negative impacts of human activities on groundwater levels and quality, the SAP advocates legal and institutional mechanisms capable of regional protection and control of groundwater extraction and of defining priority for groundwater uses. The ultimate goal is to enable – through appropriate legal and institutional procedures – transboundary cooperation and integration of aquifer-dependent socio-economic activities, including land uses, based on the efficient use of the NSAS groundwater resources and taking into account impacts on agriculture (e.g., pollution, chemical standards, industrial discharges) and on human migration flows. Migration, in particular, is spurred by dwindling livelihoods affected by lack of water. Migration and water scarcity are closely linked phenomena in general, with the latter amplifying the former, and generating what are commonly referred to as environmental refugees.

There have been no further developments regarding the SAP, due in part to the civil war in Libya. Nonetheless, as late as 2015, on the occasion of the 7th World Water Forum, in South Korea, Chad, Egypt and Sudan reiterated their intent to cooperate towards the sustainable management of the NSAS (Egypt SIS, 2015). It is to be hoped that the Government of National Accord formed in December 2015 under the aegis of the United Nations will enable Libya to resume cooperation with the other NSAS countries.

An evolutionary cooperation pattern

The cooperation pattern born of the mentioned agreements, also as regards the SAP implementation, triggers a number of considerations. First, the Joint Authority was conceived as a joint institution, but devoid of authority over the management of the shared aquifer. A careful analysis of the 1992 agreement discloses that the Authority has ample powers, but only regarding its own internal administrative organization and functioning. The only provision regarding the management of groundwater concerns the responsibilities of the Authority, listed in Article 3. Nevertheless, the 1992 agreement represents the first step on the road to cooperation, if only through its existence, particularly between the aquifer's main users, Egypt and Libya. The 1992 instrument can be regarded as the precursor to the subsequent 2000 agreements, signalling a shift from a purely 'institutional' agreement to more specific, procedural agreements covering monitoring and data exchange and data sharing. Still, the two 2000 instruments are not flawless. For one thing, their scope is restricted to information and data. Moreover, neither agreement addresses the management of the aquifer and the relevant decision-making processes (see the SAP, pp. 35–36).

The 2006 GEF-funded project was a significant milestone in the slow but steady path to cooperation in the management of the shared aquifer. Not only does the programme enable a better knowledge of the aquifer and of the relevant issues, it also lays the foundations for the SAP and for the preparation of an agreement. The programme can be therefore regarded as a preparatory agreement of the SAP. Upon closer observation, some substantive norms can be gleaned from the programme, which were absent in the prior agreements. In this connection, the SAP is one of the results of the 2006 project. SAP is a policy document to implementing actions at different points in time. Although it is not an agreement in a technical sense, the SAP is an instrument that has been subscribed to, and signed, by all parties concerned. From the programme, one can infer the intent of the parties to also prepare a convention for the management of the NSAS as the ultimate goal. Cooperation has thus been progressing stepwise, by mutually reinforcing increments, and it has reflected the principles of international environmental law, which the parties have explicitly recalled in the implementation of the SAP (GEF, 2018).

In sum, all the mentioned agreements bear out a pattern of evolving cooperation. The agreements on record so far only posit procedural norms, with no reference to substantive norms or to rules for the settlement of disputes that may arise among the parties. The need for a legally binding agreement among the four NSAS countries for the equitable and rational management of the aquifer is readily apparent from the embryonic state of cooperation to date. As one commentator puts it, 'transboundary cooperation concerning groundwater resources in the region is still in its infancy' (Alker, 2008, pp. 267–268).

The rules of international law applicable to the NSAS: the Draft Articles on the Law of Transboundary Aquifers (2008)

In this author's opinion, a legally binding treaty for the NSAS which includes substantive as well as formal and procedural norms for the agreed management of the aquifer, and for the settlement of disputes, is highly desirable, for countries may have a different view of what a future agreement says or of how it should be implemented, and may wish to map out in advance the available courses of action to deal with such situations, thus minimizing the potential for conflict. The principles posited in the Draft Articles on the Law of Transboundary Aquifers adopted by the United Nations International Law Commission in 2008 (hereinafter referred to as ILC Draft Articles, appended to UNGA Resolution No.63/124 of 11 December 2008) could point in the right direction, as regards substantive norms on equitable and reasonable use, the duty not to cause significant harm, and procedural and environmental protection norms. It would be useful to add norms for the settlement of disputes that might arise among concerned states, something which is not provided for in the ILC Draft Articles. An analysis of the draft articles and of their relevance as a template for sustained cooperation in the management of the groundwater resources of the NSAS follows.

The ILC Draft Articles

In the draft articles, an aquifer is defined as a 'permeable water-bearing geological formation underlain by a less permeable layer and the water contained in the saturated zone of the formation' (Art. 2). Thus, an aquifer has two components: the underground geologic formation which acts as a container, and the water in it. From Article 1 it is readily apparent also that the ILC Draft Articles are not limited to the utilization of aquifers; they extend to all activities that may affect the aquifers, thus extending to measures for aquifer protection, conservation and management. Aquifer 'utilization' also stretches from the withdrawal of groundwater stored in the aquifer to the extraction of heat and the exploitation of geothermal energy, to the extraction of minerals, to the underground storage and disposal of waste, all the way to the capture of carbon emissions. The balance of the ILC Draft Articles is generally patterned after the 1997 UN Convention on the Non-navigational Uses of International Watercourses (UNWC), with the appropriate adjustments dictated by the peculiar nature and vulnerability to pollution of aquifers (Quadri, 2011).

The sections that follow focus on those articles in the ILC Draft Articles which are more relevant to the NSAS context, in particular the articles regarding the equitable and reasonable utilization principle, the duty not to cause significant harm, and the protection of the environment.

Substantive norms

The substantive norms applicable to the NSAS are the equitable and reasonable utilization principle and the duty not to cause significant harm. In the ILC Draft Articles, the former is crystallized in Article 4. In particular, the article states that states 'shall utilize transboundary aquifers ... in a manner that is consistent with the equitable and reasonable accrual of benefits therefrom to the aquifer States concerned' (at letter *a*). Arguably, Article 4 also hints at the equitable and reasonable utilization of aquifers (in particular, non-recharging or 'fossil' aquifers) when it directs states to 'aim at maximizing the long-term benefits derived from the use of water contained' in all aquifers in general (letter *b*). Germane to the equitable and reasonable utilization principle, the duty not to cause significant harm is stated in Article 6 of the ILC Draft Articles. Harm may come from the utilization of transboundary aquifers, as well as from activities affecting them (6(1) and (2)). Examples of such activities include industrial and agricultural operations in the recharge zone that might pollute the aquifer; mining activities that destroy the aquifer matrix and thereby its functioning; and construction, forestry and other activities that might deplete the aquifer by preventing normal recharge. No significant harm is a fundamental principle of international water law; it is based on the Latin maxim *Sic utere tuo ut alienum non laedas*: a state should not use its territory in a way that will harm the territory of another states. Article 6 reflects hydrologic reality in requiring that significant harm be prevented, not only with respect to other states sharing a transboundary aquifer, but also with respect to those in whose territory a discharge zone is located. Given that the assessment process for aquifer contamination is more complex than for surface waters, a lower threshold may be required than that applied to surface waters. The ILC suggests that an alternative for the word 'significant' is not necessary because significance is 'a flexible and relative concept'; 'significant' should therefore be judged in relation to the totality of the circumstances. Depending on the circumstances, what might be regarded as significant in one scenario, might be considered insignificant in another (Eckstein, 2007; McCaffrey, 2009). Also, the obligation is not absolute, as under Article 6(3) a state causing significant harm may adopt suitable remedial measures. Moreover, the obligation is without prejudice to the equitable and reasonable utilization principle of shared water resources. The work of the ILC on the characterization of 'harm' is also relevant in this connection (Draft Articles on the Law of Transboundary Aquifers with Commentaries, 2008). Some ILC members had suggested lowering the threshold of harm, and thus expanding the preventive umbrella of Article 6, in view of the vulnerability of aquifers. It can be readily appreciated how relevant such an extended notion of harm is to the NSAS: because the fossil aquifer is non-recharging, it is more vulnerable to pollution and over-exploitation. Moreover, some commentators (Brooks, 2013) maintain that the no significant harm obligation should take precedence over the equitable and reasonable utilization principle in view of the vulnerability of aquifers to pollution and the near-impossibility of decontaminating a polluted aquifer.

Procedural norms

Article 13 posits the obligation of states to monitor a transboundary aquifer. To this end, states must employ agreed standards and methodologies and also exchange data and information on the state of the aquifer (Article 8). If the extent and the yield of the aquifer are uncertain, states are under a due-diligence obligation to use their best efforts to collect the necessary information, using agreed or harmonized standards and methodologies. Also in the NSAS case, procedural norms would play an important role in support of substantive norms in a hypothetical future aquifer agreement aimed at the equitable and reasonable utilization of this vital resource.

The importance of procedural norms is borne out by numerous international surface water agreements, notably the UNWC, the 1944 water treaty between Mexico and the United States governing the Colorado, Rio Grande, and Tijuana Rivers (Article 2), the 1960 Indus Waters Treaty between India and Pakistan (Article 6), the 1992 UNECE Convention on the Protection and Use of International Rivers and Lakes (Article 6), the 1996 Mekong Agreement between Cambodia, Laos, Thailand and Vietnam (Article 24), the 2000 Southern African Development Community Protocol (Article 2), the 1996 Ganges Waters Treaty between Bangladesh and India (Articles 4 and 6), the 1964 Treaty between Poland and Union of Soviet Socialist Republics Concerning Frontier Waters (Article 8), the 1971 Agreement between Finland and Sweden Concerning Frontier Waters (Article 3), and the 1975 Statute of the Uruguay River between Argentina and Uruguay (Article s7-12). As a direct reflection of the interest of states sharing an international watercourse in the mutually beneficial management and development of the water resources of that watercourse, Article 9 of the UNWC, in particular, lays down the obligation of states to exchange hydrological, meteorological, hydrogeological and ecological information and data. This procedural obligation goes hand in hand with the obligation of the same states to provide prior and timely notification of planned 'measures' that may have a 'significant' adverse effect on other watercourse states. Notification must be accompanied by available technical data and information, including the results of any environmental impact assessment (Article 12). The reciprocal obligations of the notifying and of the notified state are also regulated in detail, in Articles 13 to 17. Of particular note are the obligation of both states to consult and to negotiate with a view to reaching agreement on an equitable solution of the issue, and the obligation of the notifying state to refrain from implementing a proposed 'measure' for a period of six months, if so requested by the notified state (Article 17).

The procedural norms featured in the ILC Draft Articles do not depart in any material respect from the procedural norms posited in the UNWC. Certain nuances, however, reflecting the distinctive traits of aquifers, especially as regards their greater vulnerability and liability to overexploitation, merit attention. Article 8 of the ILC Draft Articles, for instance, is patterned after Article 9 of the UNWC. However, the information and data – geological, hydro-geological, etc. – that aquifer states are to collect and exchange are tailored to the specificities of aquifers and help delineate the aquifer's characteristics (Article 8(1)). Aquifer states are to exchange not just information and data but also 'related forecasts'. (The forecasts envisaged concern matters such as weather patterns and their possible effects on water levels and flow, the amount of recharge and discharge, foreseeable ice conditions, possible long-term effects of present utilization, and condition or movement of living resources.) The required information and data relate to the water potential and/or the chemical composition of the aquifer waters, the recharge and discharge volumes, the long-term impact of withdrawals, modelling the aquifer behaviour, etc. Moreover, in response to the far lesser knowledge and awareness that states have of their transboundary aquifers relative to the knowledge and information available regarding their transboundary surface watercourses, Article 8(2) of the ILC Draft Articles requires states to 'employ their best efforts' to fill knowledge and information gaps about the transboundary aquifers they share across international boundary lines with neighbouring states – acting individually or jointly with fellow aquifer states, and observing 'current practices and standards'. As the collection and processing of aquifer data and information can entail considerable expense, an aquifer state that is asked by a fellow aquifer state to supply data that is not readily available may condition its response on payment of 'reasonable' costs (Article 8(3)). Finally, the criticality of data regarding generally poorly known transboundary aquifers is such that data must be supplied in a format suitable for use by the aquifer state to which the data are destined. As a result, pursuant to Article 8(4), aquifer states are under the dual obligation to 'employ their best efforts' not only to collect and process data and information, but also to make them available to the requesting state in a format that facilitates their use by the latter (Eckstein, 2007). A related nuance regarding the use of the qualifier 'as appropriate' in Article 8(4) of the ILC Draft Articles, compared to Article 9(3) of the UNWC, is worth noting. Whereas the qualifier is placed before, and attenuates, the obligation to process collected data in the UNWC, that same qualifier is placed before, and attenuates, both obligations – to collect and to process the data – in the ILC Draft Articles. The net result of this less felicitous placement in the ILC Draft Articles compared to the UNWC is that information and data collected by means of one particular system may not be usable by a fellow aquifer state that employs a different system. Yet the sharing of data and information is critical to the proper management of international watercourses and to equitable utilization itself, and it is particularly critical for groundwater, about which we have less knowledge than we do about surface water (McCaffrey, 2009).

Environmental norms

'Environmental' norms are no less important in the general economy of the ILC Draft Articles, particularly in view of the peculiar nature of aquifers in general and of fossil aquifers in particular, which calls for greater protection. Article 10 carries the obligation of aquifer states 'to take all appropriate measures to protect and preserve ecosystems within, or dependent upon' transboundary aquifers they share. Measures 'to ensure that the quality and quantity of water retained in an aquifer . . ., as well as that released through its discharge zones, are sufficient to protect and preserve such ecosystems' are singled out among the measures to be taken. States therefore are under a duty to safeguard freshwater ecosystems and to protect them, with the aim to preserve to the extent possible their natural state, especially in response to external, mostly anthropogenic, interferences that may threaten the delicate balance of the constituent elements of freshwater ecosystems. Aquifer states are also under a due-diligence obligation to prevent 'new' pollution and to control and abate existing pollution that could harm other states (Art. 12).

In view of the importance of the recharge and discharge zones of aquifers, and of the relevant natural processes, to the health, functioning and viability of aquifers, such zones attract special attention in a dedicated Article 11 of the ILC Draft Articles. In accordance with the relevant definitions clause (Article 2), the recharge and discharge zones of aquifers lie outside aquifers, yet both are integral parts of the same. A recharge zone is the area that contributes water to the aquifer and includes the zone where rainwater directly infiltrates the ground, the zone of surface runoff which eventually infiltrates the ground, and the underground unsaturated zone of infiltration. The discharge zone is the area through which water from the aquifer flows to its outlet, i.e., a river, a lake, an ocean or an oasis, but such outlets are not part of the discharge zone itself. These zones, and the natural processes that occur in them, need special care to prevent or minimize aquifer pollution, in particular through the recharge zone, to maintain the functioning of the aquifer. Particularly as regards the recharge zone, protection is with a view to ensuring the volume and quality of water that flows into the aquifer. As a result, protection may include restrictions on industrial development in the recharge zone that interferes with the flow of water into an aquifer, as well as restrictions on polluting industrial and agricultural development activities in the same zone. Similar restrictions are in order as regards the protection of the discharge zones of aquifers from interference with the movement of water in an aquifer, the location of the water table, the aquifer's cleansing abilities, etc. Some scholars have rightly observed that Article 11(1) is weak, insofar as an aquifer state could deny the existence of a recharge or discharge zone in its own territory and refuse to take 'special measures' about either or both. One approach to overcoming such weaknesses, put forward by Gabriel Eckstein (2007), is through an obligation for aquifer states to cooperate with a view to surveying any recharge and discharge zone in their respective territory and taking special measures to prevent or minimize detrimental impacts on the recharge and discharge processes. This approach is consistent with the general obligation of aquifer states to cooperate, posited by Article 7, which has the effect of preventing unilateral decisions regarding a transboundary resource. Article 11(2) dwells further on the significance of the recharge and discharge zones of aquifers and on the importance of cooperation of all the states involved – both 'aquifer' and 'non-aquifer' – in whose territory such zones lie. The integrity of such zones and of the natural processes that occur in them is of such importance to the viability of a transboundary aquifer that a non-aquifer state in whose territory a recharge or discharge zone is located, in whole or only in part, is, in accordance with Article 11(2), under an obligation to cooperate with aquifer states to protect the aquifer and related ecosystems.

The principle of the limited sovereignty of aquifer states

The combined norms illustrated earlier lead to limits on the sovereignty of states sharing a transboundary aquifer. The relevant principle enables riparian states to achieve good neighbourly relations based on a 'community of interests' pursued in the utilization of shared watercourses (Rieu-Clarke, Moynihan, & Magsig, 2012). The limited sovereignty principle is enshrined in Article 3 of the ILC Draft Articles, whereby each state has sovereignty over the portion of a transboundary aquifer situated in its territory (Rieu-Clarke et al., 2012). But the exercise of this sovereignty is qualified by the rules of general international law and by those posited in the ILC Draft Articles. The second sentence of Article 3, in particular, bears out the limited sovereignty concept, as sovereignty must be exercised in conformity with international law and the ILC Draft Articles. In substance, states have sovereignty over the portion of a shared aquifer in their respective territory, yet this sovereignty is limited – attenuated by the principle of equitable and reasonable utilization posited by Article 4, by the duty not to cause significant harm posited by Article 6, and by the overall thrust of the ILC Draft Articles.

Towards a joint management of the NSAS: other possible approaches

Some commentators have argued that the NSAS cannot be used sustainably because the groundwater stocked in the aquifer, however plentiful, is non-renewable, and therefore destined for eventual depletion (Davids, 2005). In this connection, this author is of the opinion that the aquifer must be exploited for the subsistence and the economic development needs of the populations that depend on it, and that the principles enshrined in the Bellagio Draft Treaty (Hayton & Utton, 1989) provide the most suitable guidance in this regard. The Draft Treaty contemplates the eventual exhaustion of non-renewable aquifers, and in view of that, states are directed to adopt measures to slow the rate of depletion and to consider alternative sources of water. States are also invited to prioritize certain uses, notably, the satisfaction of vital human needs, and to discourage or forbid other uses. States are also called upon to agree by mutual accord on rules for the utilization of groundwater and to establish inter-state commissions with sufficient authority to manage the aquifer resources. If states followed them, arguably those norms could evolve into customary law governing non-renewable transboundary aquifers (Davids, 2005). Some observers argue that the management of fossil aquifers is best served if, instead of looking forward to *a priori* governance criteria, policy makers looked backwards to take stock of existing agreements and derive from them practical norms and criteria that appear to have worked (Lautze & Giordano, 2006). This may be true, but agreements are subject to revisitation and adaptation to changing circumstances.

Other observers (Al Eryani, Appelgren, & Foster, 2006) believe that the amount of groundwater required by development projects in Egypt and in Libya is so small relative to the total volumes stocked in the NSAS that no cross-border impact will be felt, at least in the near future. They also argue that, as a result, cooperation limited to data and information exchange is sufficient. Another author disagrees (Alker, 2008); in her opinion, management of the NSAS requires not only procedural but also substantive norms, as well as norms for the settlement of disputes that may arise among the states concerned. She agrees with those who advocate strong cooperation grounded at the political level, as this is the road to achieving optimization of social development in the NSAS region and to balancing the asymmetrical interests of the aquifer states to the north and to the south of the aquifer, respectively. As observed earlier (Alker, 2008), Chad and Sudan –the upstream aquifer states[2] – are in a weaker position than Egypt and Libya in view of the technical and economic limitations on the exploitation of the aquifer in their respective territories and in view of political stability factors. It is also true, however, that the current political instability in Libya undermines that country's position in regard to the aquifer. One commentator maintains that cooperation is a matter of strategic choice of the four countries, aimed at preventing international conflict over socio-ecoomic and environmental goals, and at ensuring access to water, particularly in a water-scarce region. Under the circumstances, therefore, cooperation is a national security issue (Alker, 2008). Another commentator (Eckstein, 2017) analyzes the possibility of directly applying the rules for liquid minerals, like oil and gas deposits, to fossil aquifers, but he highlights a number of concerns about such application: water is indispensable for life, unlike any other natural resource, which suggests that an oil/gas regime may not be appropriate; and oil/gas regimes are designed to exploit the resource in the most expedient and most efficient manner, which typically is not an objective for freshwater resources. If the notion of unitization (one manager has authority to manage and exploit the entire reserve as a single unit) used in oil/gas regimes could be interesting (Jarvis, 2011), it's also true that this is designed for their maximum exploitation, which is quite different when dealing with freshwater resources, like fossil aquifers. In contrast to the profit-driven exploitation of oil and gas, the exploitation of fossil aquifers should be driven by the need of states to satisfy the primary water needs of their populations, independent of profit motivations (Eckstein & Eckstein, 2003).

This author believes that cooperation plays a fundamental role, particularly for fossil aquifers like the NSAS. More generally, an adequate planning and governance structure is needed for the sustainable management of all shared aquifers, whether they are recharging or non-recharging. In this light, the principles enshrined in the ILC Draft Articles appear to be the most likely to ensure the sustainable management of the vital groundwater resources stored in shared aquifers in general. Moreover, other experts recommend carrying out adequate assessment and monitoring of the resources available on each side of the border to avoid any unintentional impacts to either of the countries concerned. Moreover, close cooperation between riparian countries is an essential factor in the management of transboundary aquifers (Stephan, 2009).

Conclusions

From the foregoing analysis the following conclusions can be drawn.

(1) The NSAS agreements described in this paper only address procedural norms of inter-NSAS state behaviour.

(2) The cooperation born of these agreements is a work in progress, attesting to and dependent on the willingness of the parties to embark on a path of cooperation. It has not yet reached full maturity. From an institutional-type agreement in 1992, the parties have moved on to more specific accords, laying down procedural norms in 2000. Later, the GEF programme in 2006 provided the foundations for the implementation of the SAP, which reflects a shared vision for the cooperative management of the aquifer and outlines strategies for implementation. There is still a long way to go, but cooperation is alive and kicking within the limits described in this paper.

(3) To date, the SAP has not been implemented. It is to be hoped that the formation of a stable government in Libya will enable resumption of cooperation with the other three NSAS countries, so as to bring forward what they had envisioned for the sustainable management of the NSAS at the 7th World Water Forum in 2015.

(4) The need for a legally binding agreement, providing substantive and procedural norms regulating states' behaviour, and norms for the settlement of disputes, is readily apparent. To this end, this author recommends recourse to the substantive, procedural and environmental norms featured in the ILC Draft Articles, with the addition of norms for the settlement of disputes, which the ILC Draft Articles do not provide.

(5) The ILC Draft Articles on transboundary aquifers are a step forward in the development of the international law of shared aquifers, and their provisions may be

crystallized eventually in a globally binding legal instrument. Until such a global instrument comes to pass, however, the ILC Draft Articles remain the most authoritative and articulate global-scale reference for states, as they consider the governance of the aquifers and the groundwater they share across their international boundary lines.

Notes

1. The instrument in question is styled 'Internal Regulation' in the translation into English from the Arabic original. Retrieved from http://web.cedare.org/wp-content/uploads/ 2005/ 05/Nubian-Sandstone-Aquifer-System-NSAS-Monitoring-and-Evaluation-Rapid-Assessment-Report-Final.pdf.
2. A smaller basin of the NSAS, known as the Nubian Nile aquifer, receives recharge from the Nile River; the direction of groundwater flow in the NSAS is generally from south-east to north-east. Hence, Sudan and Chad are in an upstream position, providing minor recharge to Egypt and Libya downstream (UNEP, 2007).

Disclosure statement

No potential conflict of interest was reported by the author.

References

Al Eryani, M., Appelgren, B., & Foster, S. (2006). Social and economic dimensions of non-renewable resources. In Foster & Loucks (Eds.), *Non-renewable groundwater resources: A guidebook on socially-sustainable management for water-policy makers* (pp. 25–34). IHP-VI, series on Groundwater n.10. Paris: UNESCO.

Alker, M. (2008). The Nubian Sandstone Aquifer System: A case study for the research project Transboundary groundwater management in Africa. In W. Scheumann & E. Herrfahrdt-Pähle (Eds.), *Conceptualizing cooperation on Africa's transboundary groundwater resources* (pp. 231–274). Bonn: German Development Institute.

Bakhbakhi, M. (2006). Nubian Sandstone Aquifer System. In S. Foster & D. P. Loucks (Eds.), *Non-renewable groundwater resources: A guidebook on socially-sustainable management for water-policy makers* (pp. 75–81). IHP-VI, series on Groundwater n.10. Paris: UNESCO.

Brooks, D. B. (2013). Governance of transboundary aquifers: New challenges and new opportunities. In *Global water forum*. Discussion Paper 1325. Retrieved from http://globalwaterforum.org.

Burchi, S. (2018). Legal frameworks for the governance of international transboundary aquifers: Pre- and post-ISARM experience. *Journal of Hydrology: Regional Studies, 20,* 15–20. Retrieved from https://www.sciencedirect.com

Burchi, S., & Spreij, M. (2003). *Institutions for International Freshwater Management.* UNESCO/ IHP/WWAP. IHP- VI Technical Documents in Hydrology, PC – CP series n. 3.

CEDARE. (2002). *Report centre for environment and development for the Arab Region and Europe.* Centre for Environment and Development for the Arab Region and Europe. Retrieved from http://web.cedare.org/category/wrm

CEDARE. (2014). Nubian Sandstone Aquifer System (NSAS) M&E rapid assessment report, monitoring & evaluation for water. In *North Africa (MEWINA) Project, Water Resources Management Program* (pp. 9–43). Heliopolis, Cairo: Centre for Environment and Development for the Arab Region and Europe.

Davids, J. (2005). Is it reasonable to use the Nubian Sandstone Aquifer System unsustainably under International Law? In *CEMLP annual review* (p. 9). Dundee, UK: University of Dundee.

Eckstein, G. (2007). Commentary on the U.N. International law commission's draft articles on the law of transboundary aquifers. *Colorado Journal of International Environmental Law and Policy, 18*, 3, 537–610.

Eckstein, G. (2017). Trends in the evolution of international law of transboundary aquifers. In *The international law of transboundary groundwater resources* (pp. 117–132). Earthscan Water Text Series. London: Routledge.

Eckstein, G., & Eckstein, Y. (2003). A hydrogeological approach to transboundary ground water resources and international law. *American University International Review, 19*(2), 201–258.

Egypt SIS, Egypt, Sudan, Chad to Develop Sandstone Water Reservoir. (2015). Retrieved from https://allafrica.com/stories/201504180093.html

Elbadawy, O. (2014). Arab water strategy. Paper presented at Regional Network Meeting on Water Data and Knowledge Sharing, Amman, Jordan.

GEF. (2018). Enabling Implementation of the Regional SAP for the Rational and Equitable Management of the Nubian Sandstone Aquifer System (NSAS). Retrieved from https://www.thegef.org/project/enabling-implementation-regional-sap-rational-and-equitable-management-nubian-sandstone

Hayton, R. D., & Utton, A. E. (1989). Transboundary groundwater: The Bellagio draft treaty. *International Transboundary Resources Center Natural Resources Journal, 29*(3), 663–721.

Jarvis, W. T. (2011). Unitization: A lesson in collective action from the oil industry for aquifer governance. *Journal Water International, 36*(5), 619–630.

Lautze, J., & Giordano, M. (2006). Equity in transboundary water law: Valuable paradigm or merely semantics. *Colorado Journal of International Environmental Law and Policy, 17*(1), 89–122.

Margat, J., Foster, S., & Droubi, A. (2006). Concept and importance of non-renewable resources. In S. Foster & D. P. Loucks (Eds.), *Non-renewable groundwater resources: A guidebook on socially-sustainable management for water-policy makers* (pp. 13–19). IHP-VI, series on Groundwater n.10. Paris: UNESCO.

McCaffrey, S. (2009). The International Law Commission adopts draft articles on transboundary aquifers. *American Journal of International Law, 103(2),* 272–293.

Mirghani, M. (2012). *Groundwater need assessment: Nubian Sandstone Basin.* Rio de Janeiro: WATERTRAC – Nile IWRM–NET.

Quadri, E. (2011). La complessa normativa delle falde acquifere transfrontaliere – The Law of Transboundary Aquifers: Il Progetto di articoli della Commissione di diritto internazionale. In *Gazzetta Ambiente – Rivista sull'Ambiente e il Territorio* (pp. 136–144). Anno XVII n. 4. Bologna.

Regional Action Programme for the Integrated NSAS Management (Medium Sized Project). (2006). Retrieved from https://www.thegef.org/projects

Regional Strategic Action Programme for the Nubian Aquifer System. (2013). Retrieved from https://www.iaea.org/sites/default/files/sap180913.pdf

Rieu-Clarke, A., Moynihan, R., & Magsig, B. O. (2012). *UN watercourses convention - user's guide.* Dundee: IHP-HELP Centre of Water Law, Policy and Science, University of Dundee.

Salem, O., & Pallas, P. (2002). The Nubian Sandstone Aquifer System (NSAS). In B. Appelgren (Ed.), *Managing shared aquifer resources in Africa: Regional and basin organization.* IHP-VI, series on Groundwater n.8. Paris: UNESCO.

Shared Aquifer Diagnostic Analysis (SADA). (2016). Retrieved from https://iwlearn.net/documents/11741

Stephan, R. M. (2009). *Transboundary aquifers: Managing a vital resource - the UNILC draft articles on the law of transboundary aquifers.* Edited by Raya Marina Stephan. Paris: UNESCO-IHP.

Thorweihe, U. (1990). Nubian aquifer system. In *The geology of Egypt* (2nd ed., pp. 601–614). Lisse, The Netherlands, Balkema.

UNEP. (2007). *Sudan: Post-conflict environmental assessment.* Nairobi, Kenya UNEP.

Appendix. Statutory references

Agreement No.1: Terms of Reference for the Monitoring and Exchange of Groundwater Information of the Nubian Sandstone Aquifer System, 2000. Retrieved from http://faolex.fao.org/faolex.

Agreement No. 2: Terms of Reference for Monitoring and Data Sharing, 2000. Retrieved from http://faolex.fao.org/faolex.

Agreement on Constitution of the Joint Authority for the Study and Development of the Nubian Sandstone Aquifer Waters, 1992. Retrieved from https://iwlearn.net/documents/legal-frame works/nubian-sandstone-aquifer-system-nsas.

Convention on the Law of the Non-navigational Uses of International Watercourses, 1997, entered into force 17 August 2014. See General Assembly resolution 51/229, annex, *Official Records of General Assembly, Fifty-first Session, Supplement No.49* (A/51/49). Retrieved from http://legal.un.org/ilc/texts/instruments/english/conventions/8_3_1997.pdf.

Draft Articles – The Law of Transboundary Aquifers, Resolution 63/124, adopted by UN General Assembly, 11 December 2008. Retrieved from https://www.un.org/en/ga/63/resolutions.shtml and http://www.internationalwaterlaw.org.

Draft Articles on the Law of Transboundary Aquifers with Commentaries, 2008. Retrieved from http://legal.un.org/ilc/texts/instruments/english/commentaries/8.5.2008.pdf.

Index

Note: Page numbers in **bold** type refer to tables
Page numbers in *italic* type refer to figures
Page numbers followed by 'n' refer to notes